WHY ARE WE HERE?

REFLECTIONS ON LIFE
FROM A SPIRITUAL MEDIUM

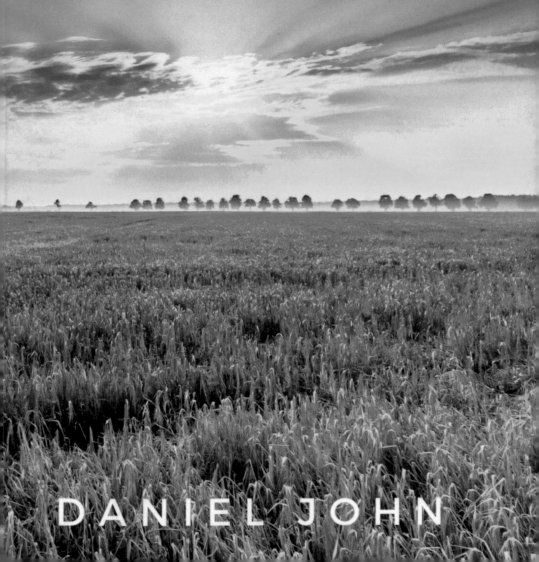

DANIEL JOHN

WHY ARE WE HERE?

REFLECTIONS ON LIFE
FROM A SPIRITUAL MEDIUM

DANIEL JOHN

WHY ARE WE HERE?

REFLECTIONS ON LIFE
FROM A SPIRITUAL MEDIUM

DANIEL JOHN

DanielJohnMedium.com

The Zome
Published in the United States of America

Scriptures quoted from the New King James Version of the Bible. (NKJV).
Copyright © 1982 by Thomas Nelson, Inc. Used by permission. All rights
reserved.

ISBN: 978-0-578-68488-8
Library of Congress Control Number: 2020907674

Printed in the United States of America
10 9 8 7 6 5 4 3 2 1

Acknowledgments

To my wife: *Alex, I would not be able to do what I do without your constant love and support. You are an amazing mother, person, and wife. Thank you for always keeping it real.*

To my mother: *Mom, thank you for all your guidance and support. Your love and presence in my life is a gift I thank God for every single day.*

To my children: *All of you make life worth living. There is nothing I would rather do than be your father. Thank you for choosing me to be your dad and giving me the love and affection I need! I love you guys!*

To my dad: *Dad, thank you! Your loving support has been crystal clear since the day I was born. You have always made me aware of your unconditional love for me.*

To "The Boys," Doozer, Istok, Darek, Dan, Nick, and Kevin: *Thank you for not thinking I am totally nuts (or if you do, for not telling me), and supporting me through all this. Your friendships are so important to me! I love you all!*

To Beth: *Spirit guided you into my life, and I am forever grateful for your constant support.*

To my spirit guides: *Thank you for being there for me in this lifetime. Thank you for your help in writing this book and thank you for always being by my side.*

To God: *I can't thank you enough for the opportunity to live this life. I am here to serve and honor You. I pledge to always listen to You no matter what anyone else says. I trust in Your guidance and will continue my mission to spread Your Love in this world!*

Once I rose above the noise and confusion,
just to get a glimpse beyond this illusion,
I was soaring ever higher. – Kerry Livgren
(From the song, "Carry On Wayward Son,"
performed by the band KANSAS).

Trust in the Lord with all your heart,
And lean not on your own understanding;
In all your ways acknowledge Him,
And He shall direct your paths.
(Proverbs 3:5-6) (NKJV)

Preface

Have you lost someone you love? Do you wonder why you are here on Earth? Ever wonder what you are meant to do while you are here? Have you ever asked yourself what happens when you die? If you answer, "Yes," to any of these questions, then you are going to love what is in the pages that follow.

I believe you are reading this book for a reason, and that in this small way, we are meant to be part of one another's journey here on Earth. I strongly believe that there is a plan for every single one of us, and part of mine is to share my spiritual discoveries with you. The sooner we open our eyes to the possibility that there is more to life than what we can see, the better off we will be. That not so transparent glimpse is what I will share with you in this book.

But who am I to be telling you this? As I write this book, I am in my late thirties with a beautiful wife and three amazing kids. I graduated high school, attended college, earned my four-year degree, and was married at the age of thirty. We started our family three years later. We live in a beautiful home on the outskirts of a small town in Upstate New York, and we have a large network of amazingly supportive friends and family. I have been a successful medical sales rep for many years, and I make a very good living.

I've had a pretty normal life on the surface of things. One exception. . .I am a medium. By that I mean I can communicate with people who have passed away. Being a medium isn't easy, and I've wanted to quit at times. It can be very draining and quite difficult, but I know that God wants me to do this work, and I'm listening to and following His direction.

The realization that I had this awesome gift didn't come to me until a few years ago, although I think it was always there. I have always had a way with people, and for a long time, I honestly thought that my normal way of being — which includes feeling other people's feelings, experiencing extrasensory perception, and just feeling things that I could not explain — was just that: Normal. I only began to pay attention to it recently, when truly out of nowhere, I gave an impromptu mediumship reading to a grieving widow at a small Italian restaurant in Boston on a cold January evening. This reading occurred at a work event and I honestly didn't even know what was happening.

It's fair to say that before I "tuned in" to my spiritual gift, I never gave mediumship much thought at all. I simply didn't believe in that sort of thing. Growing up, I went to a strict Catholic school and I thought that communicating with "the dead" was not only impossible, it was also just plain wrong. I now firmly believe that is not even close to true, as I will explain in this book.

Today, I embrace my gift as part of my life's purpose. I give readings during which I "feel," rather than see or hear, messages from Spirit. These messages help heal, give hope, and most of all, help people find, rekindle, and/or strengthen their relationship with God.

Most things in life have come easy to me, and at one time I believed that I was just "blessed" or "lucky." From serendipitous road trips, to house purchases, to job offers, I always seemed to have good things happen to me. In the pages ahead, I will share with you a few of the unbelievable "coincidences" that I have experienced, along with times when things just "fell into place." I always seemed to end up right where I needed to be.

Most importantly, by sharing what I have learned throughout my spiritual journey, I aim for this book to help you understand what forces are truly at work in this world. I firmly believe that coming from a place of love, and putting others' needs before my own, is the true reason why I've had so many blessings in my life. I feel that the things I have learned in my life experience, can be of enormous value to you in your life too. Some of them, like listening to intuition and leading with love, are things that I always did unconsciously, but only came to understand later. I will discuss how being full of love for others and listening to your heart, will guide you to your highest path. I will talk about intuition and why you should let your inner self, or "heart," guide you even when your outer self, or "ego," is telling you differently.

It may not always seem like it, but things always work out the way they are supposed to work out. Granted, there are times when we let our hearts guide us and things still don't work out the way we want them to. But even in those times, things are still as they should be, especially if you listened to your heart and came from a place of love. Through my experiences as a medium, I have come to firmly believe that the Universe (God), has a plan for every single one of us. It is a plan that is often beyond our understanding.

Each one of us comes to Earth for one, or many, specific reasons. When you discover what that is, or what they are, it can be a truly liberating experience. This book is intended for you to discover why you are here and how you can live your life on your highest path.

By sharing stories of Love and Light with you, including some of my own personal experiences, along with examples of actual mediumship readings, I aim to urge, nudge, and push you onto your highest path. By showing you how I discovered *my* life's purpose, I hope I can help you find yours, if you have not done so yet. What Spirit has shared with me about life — and the afterlife — is information intended for disseminating to others. Thank you for allowing me to share this journey of understanding with you.

Sit back, enjoy, and listen with an open mind.

CONTENTS

Chapter 1
Listen to Your Heart

Just by reading this book, you are taking a giant step on your path toward discovery. Let me get you up to speed. Throughout my life, I have experienced many synchronicities — what we often call "coincidences"— that would send chills throughout your entire body. Sharing them, along with how I found my life path, will have value for you as you navigate through your life, and find out why you, specifically, are here. I feel that our greatest challenge, while we are here on Earth, is to discover why we *are* here, and then strive to accomplish the things that will fulfill our mission.

You will notice a common theme to my experiences, and that is that I *always* listen to my heart. You will notice that I use words like "Spirit," "Universe," "God," "Him," "It," "Allah," "Love," "Light," "Source," and "One Source," interchangeably throughout this book. I believe they are all the same, and you are part of "It." You may also notice that I *intentionally* don't capitalize "satan" or "devil," or "hell," because in my opinion, they are illusions, and therefore, for me, standard grammatical propriety does not apply.

Two overwhelmingly obvious truths that I have learned

through my spiritual awakening are that *we are Love,* and *we are all One*. The sooner we recognize that we come from One Source, the sooner we can live our life to the fullest.

You know that weird feeling you have when a decision or experience just doesn't feel right? Did you ever feel a strong nudge to do, or not do, something specific? Listen to that intuition and trust it.

One of my favorite quotes from Paulo Coelho's book, *The Alchemist*, is: "Listen to your heart. It knows all things. It came from the Soul of the World and one day will return there." (Coelho, Paulo. *The Alchemist.* HarperCollins [1993], p. 127).

One of the keys to abundance in life is to trust and listen to your intuition. Your intuition is aligned with the Universe and is always right. You do not need a medium or anyone else to know God. He is within you. And He is available to us all whenever we need Him.

In the fall of 2004, I experienced one of those times where I chose to listen to the Universe (heart), and not my ego (head). What I wanted to do, and what the Universe wanted me to do, were two *very* different things. . .

My cousin, Erik, was getting married at an all-inclusive resort in the Bahamas and guess who was invited? Oh, yeah, *me!* At the time, I was in my early twenties, living at home with my mom, and making good money. So, I accepted the invitation to the wedding and bought my pricey flight and hotel package. I'm a big family guy, and I was extremely excited to go on this family trip.

After I booked the trip however, an uneasy feeling settled over me that I really can't put into words. I couldn't sleep, and I pictured a plane crash in my head every single day. This feeling that something was not right actually started to make me physically sick. I was pressed to choose between what I call an ego-based decision and a love-based decision. I would have loved to go on that trip, but somehow, I knew that it would not be a good thing if I went. I didn't understand the reason, but I felt like I had no choice but to listen to the Universe.

The stress and anxiety regarding this trip became so intense, it was almost unbearable. Finally, about a month or so before the trip, I made a radical decision. I gave the entire trip — 100% paid for — to my sister. And I agreed to babysit her son, my seven-year-old nephew, while she would be swimming up to the pool bar for refills of frozen Margarita's all day in the Bahamas. One minute I was headed to a tropical all-inclusive resort with my family, and the next, I'd committed to staying home in Upstate New York to watch a seven-year-old during a cold and rainy October. *What the heck?*

As soon as I officially changed the name on the flight and resort package to my sister's name (which went very smoothly even though it was only 3 years after 9/11), I felt a *huge* weight lifted off me. The uneasiness and fear instantly vanished. After I made the decision, I remember smiling ear to ear while looking out the window of a hotel room I was staying in for work. I can't explain how great it felt to be able to give my sister something she needed at the time. It was also refreshing that I had the trust to listen to my intuition even though it was a pretty bold decision.

My face quickly transformed into shock when I remembered one of the things that had led up to me making my decision. I thought, *Oh, no! Now, my sister, mother, and grandmother, would all be on the same flight that I had seen crashing in my mind day after day. How could I not have thought about that?*

The anxiety immediately set in again as I questioned everything that was happening. However, the fear quickly disappeared, when in that very moment, I "heard" a voice in my mind. It "said," "We used your fear of flying because you were not to go on that trip." The message was very simple, to the point, and it was very strong. It was simultaneously accompanied by a feeling of, "The plane obviously is not going to crash. They will all be safe." I still don't know who or what that "voice" was, but it was powerful and direct. It was the first of many wild and goosebump-raising moments that would lead me to wholeheartedly trust in God and His plan.

Direction from God helped me make the right decision, because my sister later said the trip was something she needed very much at that point in her life. It didn't make her happy forever, however. In fact, she has lost touch with our family for many years now. I still feel good in my heart about it, because it was a loving thing to do. She could not have afforded the ticket at the time, and I felt honored to provide something of value to her. I truly felt that I wasn't supposed to go as well, so it made sense both ways. It felt good to be able to recognize that the Universe was able to guide me in a direction that provided something that helped her so much.

To this day, I just know that something unfavorable would have happened to me, or someone else on that trip, if I had not listened to my intuition and decided to go. Maybe I would have fallen and broken my ankle. Maybe I would have met the wrong girl. *Who knows?* Maybe I would have gotten a tattoo of Dwayne, "The Rock," Johnson on my left ass cheek after a few too many tequilas. *Come on, who doesn't have a man-crush on that guy?*

Whatever may have happened, I've never questioned that I did the right thing. My family went on the trip, had a lot of fun, and most importantly, they all returned home safely after a great wedding celebration.

In this situation, I trusted my heart, acting *not on what I wanted for myself*, but instead, making a decision based on *what would be the best outcome for all involved*. This kind of approach has worked out extremely well for me many times since then.

When we take our own personal gain out of a situation and strive to help others, while serving God, the outcome leads to our highest life path. That selflessness is what leads to many blessings throughout one's life. That "voice," or "feeling," sometimes seems to contradict common sense, and stands in opposition to what we selfishly want. But you will never be led astray by listening to it. *Never.*

One fall, about eight years after that experience, I was out in my yard raking leaves, a month or so after our first son, Sammy, was born. No one else was home or even around me. That's when that same "voice" came to me again. The "voice" said, "If you quit gambling, you have a gift." At the time, I couldn't tell you what the gift could possibly be, but I surely can now. I wouldn't fully comprehend this message until about five years later.

I had been a gambler since college. I wasn't compulsive, but I used to play poker, bet on sports, and play fantasy football and baseball for money. I had tried to quit over the years and had periodic successes, but I didn't permanently quit until early 2017. This would be the year when all the pieces of my spiritual puzzle started to come together.

While driving in a major snowstorm in March of 2017, I decided to pull over and visit a casino because it was becoming too dangerous to drive. On my way inside, I called my best friend, Mike, and said to him, "If I hit the jackpot, I am finally going to quit gambling forever."

Well, while I was in the casino, I hit a royal flush on draw poker, a computerized poker slot game, and won $4,000. Then I quit, right? *Nope.* If you believe it is that easy, you don't understand how addicting gambling can be to certain people. It was just like the last ten times I had tried to quit gambling. After all, they had just built a brand-new casino with a poker room a short twenty-minute drive from our house. *I couldn't quit now, right?*

I played poker a few more times, until one night I had a bad loss and it all felt very wrong. I suddenly got real serious about quitting. I mean, I had already said I would stop gambling if I hit that jackpot, and I hadn't stuck to my word. *Now*, I realized *I had to* quit.

I went home, got on my knees in my living room, and I swore on my life, on my kids' lives, and on my soul, that I would never gamble again. I truly did quit that day. And I have not gambled since.

Although I occasionally miss the thrill of gambling, it does not compare to the healing power of the gift that was revealed to me. The next few months after I quit gambling proved to be an extremely difficult time for me. I started to develop major stomach issues and I had severe insomnia. Some nights, I think I didn't sleep at all. I started taking Benadryl® and other sleep aids regularly, and things were not going well. If insomnia wasn't enough, I had a constant lump in my throat, and I needed to see a cardiologist and gastroenterologist for a battery of tests. After two months of rigorous testing and sleepless nights, every doctor I visited said that all my issues stemmed from anxiety and stress.

During that time, I "randomly" met or ran into four or five people who recommended I try meditation. I figured I had nothing to lose, so I started meditating. I didn't know if I was doing it right, and it didn't seem to be helping much, but I stuck with it. After about one month of consistently meditating, I started to feel a little better. My symptoms were still very much there, and I still wasn't sleeping well at all. I continued to meditate over the next few months and finally, my stomach and sleeping issues started to improve. It wasn't until early fall of 2017, that my health issues improved enough to be considered minor ones.

We will delve into meditation more in a later chapter, but I want to tell you that it is important to be consistent and patient with meditation. Practice it daily, and it will be well worth it. Meditation can and will be life-changing for you.

Now, I would like to share something with you that happened a couple of months *before* I quit gambling. I had an experience that would change my life forever.

One evening, while in Boston for a business trip in January 2017, our entire group of sales reps went out to dinner for a team-building event. I ended up sitting next to a woman named Deidre. Deidre, a fun, energetic woman in her 40s, was a new member of our team. When she introduced herself to us earlier that day, she mentioned that her husband had passed away six months prior. I thought nothing at all of that as I sat next to her that evening.

As we started chatting, I started to get these visions, feelings, and pictures in my mind. This had happened to me before, but it was not even close to anything this powerful. I shared the messages I was "receiving" with her, and we conclusively confirmed that Bob, Deidre's deceased husband, was somehow communicating with us.

After about forty-five minutes of many emotional tears, and even some laughter, the "reading" was done. We hugged, as she said to me, "I have been waiting for this. Thank you so much!"

Bob's messages were subtle, in terms of my reception and understanding of them, but they were massive in their importance to Deidre. Bob had died suddenly, right in front of Deidre at their home. They never had a chance to say goodbye. This "reading" was their goodbye. And I was honored to be part of it.

Bob wanted Deidre to know he was okay and that he was still with her. Through me, he passed on many messages of love, along with very specific personal information that only she would understand. The love and specific detailed information that he communicated that evening was extremely healing for her — and I got to witness it all firsthand. Being able to help her gave me the most incredible feeling. Deidre and I are friends to this day, and she has told me that her reading had a profoundly positive effect on her life in a way she could never fully explain.

As you might guess, I realized that mediumship was something I needed to explore. Even though I was still struggling to believe and understand how it all worked, if I could use it to help people feel better, I had to investigate. I thought to myself, *Did I just read her mind or something? Did I just make all this stuff up? Were they lucky guesses? Where was that stuff coming from?* All the information was so accurate and specific to her and her family. *Really. . .what happened that night?*

Being a skeptic by nature, I didn't know what to think. I knew that I loved helping Deidre, and I have always enjoyed helping people throughout my entire life. I didn't tell anyone about my experience with Deidre for at least a few months. I didn't even tell my wife or my mom, and believe me, I tell them *everything.* I didn't even know how to begin to tell anyone. I felt anxious about what people might say, so I kept it to myself. However, I did not keep it quiet for long.

After this experience, I had what I would call a "craving" to watch shows featuring mediums. I watched hours and hours of shows like *Long Island Medium* with Theresa Caputo, *The Hollywood Medium* with Tyler Henry, and *Crossing Over* with John Edward. I bought and read many of their books, along with those of other mediums as well.

Although my free time was limited with work and our three little kids, I spent a great deal of it watching mediumship readings. In 2017, I read at least fifty books on mediumship, life after death, near-death experiences, and God/the Universe. I devoured every metaphysical or spiritual nonfiction book I could get my hands on.

It's so important to note that each time I felt guided to a book, I asked God if it contained truths that He wanted me to understand. I also asked that He warn me if the book was not of His Love. Sometimes the answer was *no*, and sometimes it was *yes*. Sometimes I picked up a book and I felt part of it was truth and part of it was not. All the same, I leaned not on my own understanding, but on God and His direction. (Proverbs 3:5–6).

Before this, I had never really had a solid belief surrounding the afterlife. I was raised Catholic, then became a "saved" Christian in high school. I always believed in God and Jesus, and while I was in college, I taught religious education at a Catholic church as a volunteer. I just thought that we went to Heaven or hell and that was it.

As I continued to watch readings by mediums on TV, not only did I begin to believe that they were real, I was struck by the powerful healing and love that was shared through them. The people receiving the readings, or what mediums call "sitters," were so happy, and positively affected by their mediumship reading experience. The sitters often received messages of love, forgiveness, compassion, and hope. They found so much peace in the fact that their loved ones could communicate messages of love to them, while also informing them that they are still very much a part of their lives, and above all, letting them know that they are not "dead."

After learning about mediumship by reading and watching shows, I decided to make an appointment of my own with a local medium to explore whether or not this "medium stuff" was all legit. Being a natural skeptic, I needed to see mediumship in action for myself to believe it was real and not just a hoax. I booked an appointment with Beth, a well-known and very respected medium in our local area.

Even though I had delivered a reading of my own to Deidre in Boston just a few months before, I was still quite skeptical of the whole thing. After the reading with Beth, that lasted well over an hour, I was now a believer. I must have listened to the recording Beth provided me about twenty or thirty times afterward, because it was full of messages from my dad who had passed away a few years prior in 2014.

There were also many other messages from passed loved ones. I am not kidding when I tell you that there were things in the reading that Beth could not possibly have made up or found out. I won't list the thirty or so validations she gave me, but one in particular comes to mind. She said, "Ida says *Hi!*" Ida was my grandmother's name. She had a different last name than mine, she passed away in 2006, and she is nowhere to be found on any social media platform or search engine. It's not as if her name were "Mary" or "Marie," which can pop up eight or nine times in an Italian family tree like mine.

I had so many questions. *Where were my dad and grandma when they were communicating with Beth? Weren't they in Heaven or hell? How did Beth "hear" them?* She told me so many specific things about my family and about me, it was impossible not to believe it was real. Oh, and by the way, Beth also told me I would soon begin doing the same work that she does as a medium. After that reading, life took on a whole new meaning for me.

Over the next year, I had many synchronistic hard-to-believe experiences, some of which I will share with you in later chapters. From phone calls, to repeating number sequences, from e-mails, to songs I heard, the signs were all around me. Now that I was meditating, I was more receptive and better equipped to pay attention to them.

Today, I have fully embraced my mission as a medium. I am what is known as an evidential medium, meaning that I get very specific detailed information from Spirit. With guidance from God, I am now also a Reiki master, I have taken astrology classes, and I have read well over one-hundred metaphysical books, including the Bible. I meditate daily and receive Reiki and acupuncture treatments regularly. I have given well over eight-hundred readings — many of them for free — and I love and appreciate the gift that God has given me.

I honestly think the knowledge I have gained over the last few years can be of significant benefit to many people. I am writing this book, with nudges from God and my spirit guides, to help you as much as I can while I am here.

I feel strongly that good mediums with pure intentions, can make a dramatic difference in people's lives. To someone who is grieving a significant loss, the peace of mind they get from understanding that their loved one in spirit, is not in "hell," and is still very much with them, can have a significant impact on that person's quality of life.

The knowledge that we live on after our physical body

dies, can provide so much value to us as human beings, and it can make the world a better place. Spirit always comes through with messages of love, healing, forgiveness, and compassion. It is all about love, and only love, because that is who and what we are made of: *Love.*

Remember, I was as skeptical as anyone about mediumship. And although it's good to be skeptical, it is just as important to be open-minded. Some of the things I have learned may seem extremely hard to believe, especially if your long-standing beliefs are deeply rooted. I can tell you that the things I will share with you throughout this book are not proven facts. They are, however, what I sincerely believe to be true, given all I have experienced and researched. We all have our own beliefs, and I am not trying to change yours at all. I just want to introduce some spiritual possibilities to you as you read this, so you can investigate them yourself.

I hope that as you read what I have learned along my path, you will be encouraged to look beyond what seems to be "real," and strive to obtain a deeper understanding of your life. I think it is important to respect other people's beliefs and lead with love, even when those beliefs differ from our own.

To me, one of the most gratifying things in life is to help another human being. Holding the door, letting someone in the lane ahead of me while driving, or just smiling at a stranger, is a sign of love that I choose as often as I can.

As a medium, I feel blessed to experience God's Love in every single reading. My first reading with Beth guided me to my highest path, and I aim to do the same for all my sitters, and also for you.

Knowing for certain that my dad is still watching over me, and that life continues after we "die," has helped me be the best me I can be. I want that for you too. My job is to lift people up, give them hope, and most importantly, increase trust and faith in God, so they can experience His Love on a daily basis. Whether you are a true believer or a true skeptic, I would like to gently remind you to proceed with an open mind. *Let me help you understand why we are here.*

Chapter 2
Two Crazy Stories

I'd like to share two stories with you that may seem unreal, hard to believe, exaggerated, or even just simply made up. At the time these events occurred, I was still a major skeptic about life after death, and I constantly needed validation. These experiences, along with many others just like them, guided me to my highest path. That is the path I walk on today and every day.

I stand behind these stories and have even shared some of them at my live events and on my show, "Monday Night Live with Daniel John." (You can witness free readings and be part of the love every Monday evening, at 9 PM Eastern time, on my Facebook page, "Daniel John Medium"). I present the following stories as real, accurate, genuine, and full of God's Love.

About one month after I stopped gambling, and a month or so before I went to see a medium for the first time, I fell asleep in my daughter Stella's room. That night I had a vivid, lucid dream of my grandmother. Grandma Lori and I were very close, especially toward the end of her life. In the dream, at first, she just stood there without saying a word.

I said to my Grandma Lori with my thoughts, "Grandma, if this is really you, tell me something specific, so I can know this is real." She returned my thought with her thought, "Tell your mom I know about the teapot." *What in the world could that possibly mean?* I woke up the next morning thinking I had just made it all up in my head.

The next day, my mom came over to visit. Now, at this point, I still had not told *anyone* about the reading with Deidre in Boston. Also, remember, that although I tell my mom and my wife everything, I had chosen to keep the fact that I had communicated with a dead person to myself, even though my mom's side of the family has always had a "connection" to the other side, to say the least.

Even so, I said to my mom, "Mom, Grandma came to me in a dream last night and told me to tell you something." At this point, I still wasn't convinced about the afterlife myself, and I still wasn't sure that people who had passed away, should, or even could, communicate with us. I needed my mom to confirm that Grandma Lori really did visit me that night so I could know it was real. I was extremely disappointed when my mom said she had no idea what I was talking about.

"I don't know anything about a teapot. I'm sorry, Dan."

I was so upset because that had to mean that this vivid and lifelike experience was just a dream and nothing more. *Was there really no validity to it? How could it not have been real? It was so vivid!*

A minute or so later, as I was sulking, my mom

suddenly spoke up. "You know. . .I just changed my Amazon password."

Uninterested, I rolled my eyes. "*Well*, what did you change it to, Mom?"

"Teapot."

My jaw dropped. "Are you kidding me, Mom? You didn't think of that when I said "teapot" to you just a couple minutes ago?"

"No. It's kind of funny too," she said. "I was sitting in my kitchen and had a moment as I looked around the room trying to find something to change my password to. I looked at the teapot and changed my password to "teapot99" just last week."

Note: *In 1994, my mother had a major stroke that almost took her life. She sometimes has a difficult time remembering certain things, as well as expressing her thoughts into words. My mom is the most selfless, loving, sensitive, caring woman I have ever met. She has recovered from her stroke very well. I am so blessed to have her in my life, and I am happy that she is still here and is such a wonderful grandmother to our children.*

I was so excited! The dream was validated! I couldn't believe it! Of all things, "teapot?" It showed me that somehow, it really was the soul of my grandma that visited me in my dream that night, and she *did* communicate with me.

My grandma was confirming that she was with my mom at the time she was having a "memorable moment," not even a week prior. That kitchen table, where Mom had been sitting at in that "moment," was where she and my grandmother sat together almost every day for many years. Grandma was letting her daughter know she was still with her.

This was exactly the confirmation I needed. We *can* communicate with passed loved ones and they *can* give us messages of love. As a bonus, it was nice to know that I could connect with my grandma, with whom I had been very close.

Just to make this story even crazier, I went back into my bedroom, and in my mind, I said to my grandma, "Just show me a feather and then I'll know for sure this is real." I went out into the living room and sat with my mom, discussing how amazing this experience was. Wouldn't you know, a feather floated between her and me for about twenty seconds. It was one of the most awesome experiences I'd had up to that point in my life. This was just the beginning of the journey that I am still on today.

The next validating experience I had was just as crazy, and even more powerful. A few months after the visit from Grandma, and a couple of months after I had visited Beth, the medium, something very significant happened. It is a little complicated to explain, but I am sharing it with you to demonstrate how real both synchronicity and divine alignment are. So please, read this story slowly and thoroughly.

One night, I had a dream of my father, who had passed away a few years earlier. I will talk a little more about Dad later in this book, but for now, just know that in this dream, he randomly showed me three, very large, orange stars.

The next night, while outside in my backyard, I was on the phone with my mother. I was telling her about the dream I had of my dad the night before. At that exact moment, I actually saw three, large, orange-looking, stars in the sky. *How weird was that?*

At the exact moment I'd seen the stars, my phone alerted me that I received an e-mail from a distant uncle of mine who happens to be an astrologer. His e-mail was regarding a movie night that was planned in Seattle that upcoming weekend. What struck me about this, however, was that not only did he write me as I was looking at the stars — while talking to my mom about a dream I'd had about stars — I had recently looked into taking a class in astrology. At that time in my life, I started to become interested in astrology. This particular uncle, who I have only met a few times, had previously given me an intriguing, spot-on, astrology reading about my life based on the time and location that I was born. It was so accurate and detailed that I wanted to investigate how it all worked.

To recap. . .I had a dream in which my dad showed me stars. While on the phone with my mom telling her about that exact dream, I saw three orange stars in the sky. And at the same time, my uncle, the astrologer, sent me an e-mail about a movie showing in Seattle. . .*Got it?*

To add another layer to this story, I will explain two more synchronistic things that occurred. They were connected, but independent of all this at the time.

The first thing is that after my uncle gave me an amazing astrology reading, I looked up an astrology class online and I was a bit disappointed to find that it would cost $1,200. *That's a lot of money,* I thought, and I wasn't sure if I could justify it. At that point, I said to myself, *If my wife asks me for something that costs $1,200 or the Universe gives me exactly $1,200 somehow, that will be a sign that I should take the astrology class.*

The second independent thing that happened was I had mentioned to my wife, months earlier, that I wanted to buy her some jewelry because it had been a while. These two circumstances that had arisen independently, weeks apart, came into focus the same night I'd been on the call with my mom, telling her about the dream about stars. *Still with me?*

I was lying in bed with my wife that evening as I was going over in my head how crazy the day had been. To be telling my mom about the dream of my dad with the stars, and then to see the stars simultaneously in "real life," all the while getting an e-mail from my astrologer uncle, at that very moment, had been incredible.

Then, as I was starting to fall asleep, out of the blue, my wife said, "Is $1,200 too much for a necklace?"

"Are you kidding me?" I said, as I jumped out of the bed.

"Never mind. I was just asking," she said, annoyed.

She couldn't have known about the class being $1,200,

and what I had said to myself about it weeks before. I explained the whole thing to her, and she said, "Well, I guess you have to take an astrology class then, huh?"

I sat there in complete awe of all the coincidences that had just occurred. I almost couldn't believe it.

Then, for some inexplicable reason I said to myself, *If the headquarters of the company that sells that piece of jewelry my wife inquired about, is located in Seattle, where the movie is playing that my uncle e-mailed me about, then that would be absolute proof that I need to take an astrology class.* (Which, by the way, was something I never would have imagined doing before these events occurred). I don't know how or where this thought came from, but it did.

"That necklace is a little expensive, isn't it?" I said to my wife. "What website are you looking at, anyway?"

"Nordstrom."

"Where is Nordstrom located?"

"Why?" she asked, looking annoyed again.

"I was just wondering. Where is their headquarters?"

"Let me check," she said.

As she was looking it up, I thought to myself, *Man, I pushed it too far.* The Universe had made it pretty clear that It wanted me to take an astrology class. And now I was asking for too much validation. Besides, what were the chances that Nordstrom was located in Seattle, of all places? As I silently wished I hadn't pushed it that far, my wife finally found the answer on her phone.

"Seattle, Washington," she said.

I cannot tell you how fast and obnoxiously I jumped out of our bed again. "Oh, my God!" I said. I had goosebumps from head to toe and almost woke our four-month-old, who was sleeping in the rocker next to the bed.

"If my body wasn't covered in goosebumps right now, I would yell at you for almost waking the baby. What in the world is going on?" my wife asked.

I told her the whole unbelievable story. We were both in such awe, and it took me hours to get to sleep that night. Even though I still haven't bought my wife that expensive piece of jewelry, I did end up taking an astrology class, although it wasn't the one for $1,200. I hadn't known it at the time, but it turns out that my uncle, the astrologer, actually teaches astrology too, so I took *his* course. Talk about synchronicity! (My uncle's astrology services, Ray Couture's Astrology consultations: https://astrologicalperspectives.net).

The reason I wanted to share these two stories with you, is to illustrate how extremely beneficial it can be to pay attention and listen to what the Universe is trying to tell you. I believe there is a perfect combination of free will and destiny at work in the world, and if we pay attention, they can both lead us to our highest path in life. I *could* have gone to the Bahamas, but something (or someone), told me not to go. And I listened. I might not have taken that astrology class after all the "coincidences" I experienced, but I paid attention, trusted, and did what I was guided to do.

I urge you to listen to your heart because God speaks through it. There is a great difference between thinking and acting with your head and listening and taking action with the love in your heart. Learning the difference between them is one of the challenges we have while we are here on Earth. Pay attention and trust.

Chapter 3
The Real You

If you want to understand why you are here, one of the most important concepts you must internalize is that you are a soul living in a human body. As souls, we incarnate here to learn, and Earth is our classroom. This human experience helps our true selves — our souls, or sparks of God — grow closer to Him, which is where I believe we come from. "Source" is who and what we are made of. I often say that the "Grand Design" is truly beyond our understanding. After all my research, readings, and experiences, I feel very confident that the best way to put it is that we are Love.

Another important reason to understand that your true nature is as a soul, rather than just a human being, is that things are vastly different from the soul perspective. What seems to be "bad" or "evil," most often is just not so from the soul's point of view. As souls, we are naturally loving, compassionate, forgiving, patient, intelligent, and intuitive. When we incarnate, however, we not only develop an ego, but we lose the knowledge of who we truly are. Discovering who we really are while we are in human form is part of the challenge of life.

You might be skeptical about this, and that's okay. It is good to be skeptical, because if we weren't, we would just believe everything that is presented to us. Being open-minded, however, is just as important. You are being open-minded right now by reading this book, and that is a good thing. I tell my clients that one of the most important things in life is to trust in God and to trust in your heart, or your "gut instinct." Call it what you'd like, but there is a higher level of knowing that guides and directs us while we are here. A man's (or woman's) heart plans his (or her) way, but the Lord directs his (or her) steps. (Proverbs 16:9).

There is no death for the soul, and therefore, since we *are* eternal souls, death does not exist. In my opinion, one of the greatest teachers the Earth has ever seen, religion aside, is Yeshua, or what most people call Him: Jesus Christ. One of His main messages was, and is, to show us that we live even after we "die." He was crucified and rose from the dead. This action allows us to start to understand that we are more than just a body. We are eternal souls.

I feel that the concept of eternity is beyond human comprehension. From a human perspective, we believe there must be a start and a finish, a beginning and an end. From the perspective of the soul, we (energy), have always *been* and always will *be.* I understand that concept can be hard to grasp.

My understanding of why we are here in this life is this: We are all energy. As energy, we are sparks from one Source. As sparks of energy, we have somehow misinterpreted who we are — for what reason, I do not know — and our goal is to "rediscover" who we truly are as souls. We are Love.

The Earth is one of many planets we, as souls in physical form, can choose to "inhabit" in order to grow and learn. What I have come to understand is that we have an outline or plan of possibilities and probabilities of what this earthly life will entail. The vast number of possibilities while we are here, are all part of the "Grand Design." Throughout our earthly life, we can use our free will to help us accomplish what we came to learn. When we discover who we are while in physical form, we can grow closer to God and then realize that we never left Him.

The more you can live your daily life being kind, spreading love, forgiving, having compassion, giving thanks and appreciating God, the higher the path you will be on, and the better chance you will have of fulfilling the mission your soul has come here to accomplish.

When I started to understand that everyone in this world is made up of a larger part of themselves (their soul), it changed my perspective on life. When you realize that we all come from something greater, and that we all come here to learn, you become more patient and loving toward others, because we are all in this together.

By writing this book, I am hoping to enable you to remember who you truly are, and remind you that you came here for one, or many, specific reasons. Call it a spiritual awakening if you want, but my intention is help you wake up.

Right now, I would like you to reach up to your higher self — your soul — and ask what it is that you are to accomplish, and why specifically you are here on this Earth? After you ask this question, you may be surprised what you sense, feel, or even hear. The feeling you have inside that guides you is your higher self, and it will direct you if you pay attention. Every single one of us also has one or more spirit guides, as I will discuss in a later chapter.

For now, simply ask your higher self, "What can I do to be on my highest path?" and, "What did my soul come here to learn?" What you hear, feel, or sense, will be of great value. It could be instant, or it may take days, weeks, or even months, but know that what you are receiving is real. Pay attention. Trust the information you obtain. To help you further, I've also included a "Find Your Purpose" exercise on page 121.

Chapter 4
You Are Energy

As human beings, we are energy. I have researched this extensively and have discovered that this concept is simple, yet also complex. Once you accept the fact that you are energy, every single experience you have will take on a whole new meaning.

The most important reason to grasp this fact is because there are things that can affect us which cannot be seen with the naked eye. There are many books on the topic of human energy, but I am just going to give you an overview.

The human body consists of seven main energy portals, traditionally called *chakras*. These energy portals are responsible for the distribution of life energy, or *prana*. The seven chakras are: Root, Sacral, Solar Plexus, Heart, Throat, Third Eye, and Crown. They start at the bottom tip of the spine with the Root chakra and move throughout the midline of the body to the top of the head with the Crown chakra. I won't focus too much "energy" on the chakras here. I just want to give you some basic knowledge, so you can start to better understand how our bodies work energetically.

"The mystery of the seven stars which you saw in My

right hand, and the seven golden lampstands: The seven stars are the angels of the seven churches, and the seven lampstands which you saw are the seven churches." (Revelation 1:20). (NKJV).

As I started my awakening process, I was introduced to something called Reiki. Reiki is a technique that uses life force energy to encourage the natural healing of the body. If this is new to you it might sound crazy. I know that when someone first told me about it, I thought, *Okay. . . sure.* With further exploration however, I discovered that Reiki is something that has been proven to heal people from some significant ailments.

Sometimes, it just takes a little exploration and willingness to learn about things outside your comfort zone to understand a "reality" that might seem farfetched, or even impossible. That is what I have been doing over the last few years, so I am better able to help others. During this time, I have discovered things like Reiki — and communicating with Spirit — that I would *never* have believed were possible before.

The basic principles behind Reiki are that we are all made of energy, and we all have the ability to heal ourselves as well as others. Unfortunately, due to influences like grief, stress, anxiety, ego, diet, and lack of knowledge, we may not always be able to heal ourselves energetically. If this is the case for you, it may be advantageous for you to seek out an acupuncturist or Reiki practitioner. I mention Reiki and acupuncture together because they both work on the same premise that we are energy, and they are both non-traditional treatments, at least here in the West. They are both effective, and can be quite beneficial, especially when used in conjunction with each other.

I became a Reiki Master through a three-day-long course in 2018. As I was going through it, I was completely skeptical about the whole thing. I can now say that from the time I first practiced on people during training, to today, when I give Reiki treatments more regularly, my ability to use life force energy to help people heal from various ailments has become apparent.

I firmly believe that a lot of our diseases ("dis-eases"), ailments, and stresses, can be cured without prescription medications. I acknowledge that modern pharmaceuticals and technologies are needed. I do feel, however, that there are times when other, preventative, non-traditional, therapeutic actions, can be taken independent of, or in conjunction with, traditional medicine. Try incorporating Reiki, acupuncture, and/or meditation, as part of your routine. By doing so, you will feel better and consequently operate at a higher vibration. As we navigate through our lives, our bodies take on a lot of stress. Work, relationships, diet, and many other factors, influence our energy, and this energy has a likelihood of building up. I remember when I went to my first acupuncture appointment. As my acupuncturist, Sarah, placed the needles in the spots she needed to, I could not even speak. Not only did I not want to talk, I couldn't, even though I have the gift of gab. Afterward, I asked her what that phenomenon was, and she replied, "Thirty-seven years of built-up stress." Reiki, acupuncture, and meditation have all changed my life in a way I cannot explain. Now, I am more patient and more aware. In fact, in combination, I think they have made me a better father and husband. I don't even have road rage anymore, which is astounding, because I drive over one-hundred miles a day for my full-time job, and there are some very bad drivers out there. I can say that I am a patient man for the most part. Don't get me wrong, I do have my moments. But I am much more patient as a result of implementing these practices. You will find that you will be too.

Knowing that you are energy, and that many external things can affect you, is a big step in your evolution as a soul and as a human being. It is very important to take care of yourself energetically, because there is a balance we can maintain that allows us to be who we are as love.

Please consider nurturing yourself energetically by investigating other possible treatments for health problems, sleep issues, anxiety, and stress. Again, I'm not saying that modern medicine is unnecessary. I am merely suggesting that you explore alternative, non-traditional energy treatments for any of the common health issues you may face in your life.

As a medium, protecting myself energetically is one of the most important things for me to do. I cannot emphasize enough how important it is to ask God for protection before, during, and after readings. From what I understand, some energies are "of the Light," and others that choose — because we have free will even in soul form — not to be. Even as I make that statement, I realize how crazy these ideas would have sounded to me just a few short years ago. However, again, protecting your energetic field is extremely important.

The best way to protect yourself from any energies that are not within God's Light is to say a simple prayer. I will give you an example of what I use, but please know that you do not need specific words, because it is the intention that counts. I usually say something like:

Dear God, please protect everyone in this room with your White Light of Love. Please allow only energies of your Light to communicate with me and with everyone here. Please surround us with Your Love and only allow messages of love that are for everyone's highest good.

Whether you are reading this book because you want to practice mediumship or not, I highly recommend that you protect yourself at all times with some form of prayer. If you don't, you will open yourself up to other energies that can have a negative effect on you or your clients. During any form of mediumship, I highly recommended that you do not mess with energy that is not of the Light.

Another thing you should consider is to protect yourself from what I call "energy vacuums." These are incarnate (living) people who will suck the energy right out of you. Do you have a friend who, whenever you get off the phone with them, you find yourself having to take a deep sigh, or maybe you feel as if you have a lump in your throat? Do you get stressed in large crowds or feel uncomfortable when you look at or interact with someone who has anxiety? Whether you do or not, it may be a good idea to protect yourself with a prayer like the one I've mentioned here. Even if you don't experience these feelings, just being aware of energy and how you can protect yourself from negative forms of it, can be extremely beneficial to you.

There are situations in which you may need to avoid certain people who drain or negatively affect your energy. It's not always easy when you find yourself negatively impacted energetically by someone who you *must* be around. When you can, respectfully avoid being in their presence. However, if you *must* be around them, simply smile and say a protection prayer to yourself. You can pray something like:

God, please send Love to (the person). Please keep me in your Light of Love during my time around (the person). Remind me throughout this time with (the person), that they are a soul of Love, and allow me to be impervious to any negativity they might emit. Your Love and Light on us all!

Again, the exact words are not important, but the intention is paramount. Throughout all your life experiences, I highly recommend coming from a place of love, regardless of the person involved or the situation. This will keep your vibration high, help you to be more aware, and in turn, will help keep you resistant to negative energy.

This has been a simple overview of energy, as there

are many resources available that are dedicated to subjects like Reiki, chakras, and energy in general. I touched upon the energy basics here, because just being aware of it, can offer a significant benefit to your life experiences. Understanding that you are energy is imperative for your growth as a soul. Always remember that you are energy. Protect yourself and be aware.

Chapter 5
Meditation 101

Meditation has been around for thousands of years. It is something that has been proven to help with anxiety, pain, patience, stress, mood, overall health, awareness, and so much more. I cannot tell you how beneficial it is to include meditation as part of your daily routine. I have been meditating almost daily for about two years, and I can proudly say that I am more patient, healthy, aware, and loving, because of this simple activity.

Now don't get me wrong. Even after two years of practice, I feel as if I'm still not very good at meditation. That's okay, because it is all about intention. If you are just starting out, you can try meditation apps like Headspace™, or Calm™, or the new Spa Meditations™.

Here is a simple explanation of how I choose to meditate: Find a place where you will not be disturbed. I know firsthand this may not be easy — we have three kids, age six and under — so I understand that it can be quite difficult to find any personal time at all, much less, time to meditate. It is beneficial to meditate in the same place and at the same time of day, but it isn't necessary, as you will see benefits wherever and whenever you do it. A consistent time, like first thing in the morning or right before bed, is ideal.

I think getting comfortable is more important than trying to get into a pose that might be uncomfortable. You should try not to fall asleep during meditation, and for that reason, it may be best not to lie down. However, if you are more comfortable that way, it will still do the job. Remember, it is all about your intention.

Once you are in your "place," meditation is the easy part — or so they say. Here is what I recommend: Close your eyes and focus 100% of your attention on your breathing. It is very hard not to think about anything else but do your best to give *all* your attention to your breath. Breathe in slowly and let it out like a sigh. As you let out the sigh, let your body sink deeply into the space that you are in and let go. Breathe in again, in the same way, while focusing solely on your breath. Slowly breathe out. Thoughts *will* come into your head, and in fact, many thoughts will. Thoughts like: *I forgot to let the dog out* or *I have to pick up milk* are very normal.

Recognize when you are not focusing on your breath anymore and be aware that you are instead focusing on the thought about the milk or the dog. Acknowledge the milk or dog thought. Then release it with no emotion (a smile is okay) and bring your focus back to your breath. It is that easy.

It doesn't have to be any more complicated than that. You may find that you will have to repeat this process many times throughout a meditation session. There are many detailed books available on meditation, but even if you just begin with this simple method, you will start to see many benefits. Consistency is key.

One of the other major reasons I feel meditation should be part of everyone's daily routine is because when we relax our minds, we give ourselves a much-needed break from thinking. When we do that, we open ourselves to the possibility of receiving very useful information from the spirit world. I know, I know, it sounds crazy, but don't you find it interesting that most, if not all, mediums meditate?

When the Universe first "slapped me in the face" with meditation, I didn't even know it was a tool that mediums use to connect with Spirit. When I first considered meditating, I thought my interest in it was completely independent of my sudden interest in mediumship.

As a medium, meditation is an essential tool for tuning in to the spirit world. Meditation must be a part of my daily routine so I can relax my mind. This allows me to be more open to communication from Spirit. I am naturally the kind of person who overthinks things and it can be quite difficult for me to relax my mind. Meditation is something that not only helps my mediumship, it also helps me to be a better husband, friend, employee, and most of all, an awesome dad. I am more patient with, and aware of my kids, thanks to meditation.

Meditation is one of those things that can be very difficult to be consistent with. Finding the time and place to meditate isn't easy. I can't emphasize to you enough how beneficial it will be for you to make meditation part of your daily routine. Even if it is just for five minutes, the rewards that come from this daily dedication are bound to surpass your expectations.

If you fall off the wagon and forget to meditate for a few days, or haven't made the time for it, forgive yourself and continue right where you left off. There are days when I simply forget my daily meditation and I remember only when I am lying in bed, too tired to go downstairs to meditate. In those cases, I just close my eyes and meditate myself to sleep. I listen to my breath and focus all my attention there. It isn't ideal, but it still does the job.

Don't be hard on yourself. Even as a medium, occasionally I'll forget to meditate one, two, or even three days in a row. I forgive myself and start up again the next day with a smile on my face. Meditation is something that will always be there for you and it can only help you and the people around you. And the best part is. . .it's free!

Don't get discouraged if the benefits of meditation take some time for you to notice. Be patient with the process and trust that by practicing meditation, you are doing a great thing, not just for you, but for your family, and everyone you engage with throughout your day. It took many months after I began meditating to see a change in my anxiety and sleeping issues. I did see a significant difference in my daily life — especially when it came to patience — after just a few weeks of practicing consistently. It wasn't long after I started meditating that my wife and close friends saw a dramatic change in my demeanor. So, start meditating today. I feel very confident you will not regret it.

Chapter 6
Religion and Mediumship

Growing up, my beliefs about God were shaped by the religion my family practiced. I attended a Catholic elementary school and was a regular attendee at Catholic church on Sunday. I was baptized, received communion, gave penance, and was married in the Catholic church. I was "saved" in ninth grade, and I taught Catholicism in college. Our children are baptized and all of them have godparents.

The topic of religion is a sensitive one. It has been a major source of debate over the years, and it has resulted in severe conflict among people. As such, I do not mean to offend anyone by including this chapter. My intention is simply to share what I have learned and what I believe, based on my faith, research, and studies. I can hardly avoid talking about religion while talking about why we, as human beings, are here on Earth.

Instead of getting into theology and comparing religions, I'm going to talk about this subject from my own perspective. It wouldn't be fair for me to speak intelligently of other religions because I am not a theologian. Personally, I've only experienced Christianity, and have only done some basic research on a few of the other major world religions. I would never in any way try to change anyone or make them believe what I believe. I am just sharing my beliefs and what I have come to understand about religion and the role it plays in our society.

According to *Merriam-Webster Dictionary*, religion is "the service or worship of God or the supernatural" or "a personal set or institutionalized system of religious attitudes, beliefs, and practices." (Merriam-Webster.com, 2011, https://www.merriam-webster.com, 8 May 2011). No matter what religious background you have, I feel, in general, that religion can be a very good foundation from which to understand who we are and where we come from. Church can be great, and religion can be wonderful as well. It can also be beneficial to have an open mind and take a step back to re-examine how you look at religion. My own personal definition of religion is: "A specific set of beliefs and actions that recognize and celebrate a higher source."

Did you know there are over 4,000 religions in the world? (According to www.adherents.com). The five major global religions are: Christianity, Islam, Judaism, Buddhism, and Hinduism. Each one has its own core beliefs, and they can be very different from one another, but they also have many similarities. The major common theme among most religions is love. In my opinion, love is the single most powerful thing in this world.

When someone asks me what religion I am, I respond

with, "I am Love." You will notice throughout this book, I capitalize "Love" when referring to God's Love, because I believe that God *is* Love. I believe that "love" is the best word in our limited language to describe who we are and what we come from. We *are* Love, we are to *be* Love, and *act* as Love. In my opinion, anything other than love is not of God. I believe that each one of us is a spark of God. I believe that if we lead with love at all times, we please our Source.

With thousands of religions in the world, I honestly believe that no single one of them is right, therefore by default, making all the others wrong. If we could all accept the fact that each one of us has our own beliefs about God, the world would be a lot more peaceful. Again, I firmly believe that most religions, which are just sets of beliefs about God, are rooted in this shared concept of love. Things like tithing, treating others nicely, being thankful, acknowledging Source, praying, and personal sacrifice, are ideals held by most religions.

Religion aside, I believe there have been many souls who have incarnated here on Earth to show us our way Home. Jesus was one of them. According to Scripture and historical records, Jesus was a prophet who was thought to be free of sin and full of Love. He healed the sick and performed miracles. If you ask a Christian why Jesus incarnated here, they will likely say that He "died for our sins." I believe that both His death and ascension were to show us that we do not die, we do not need our physical bodies, and that earthly temptations or possessions do not serve us or God. I also believe that one of Jesus' greatest lessons was to teach us that love is the only way. I believe He is the perfect role model and He is who I choose to mimic while I am here. That is just my opinion about one of the most influential human beings ever to have walked the Earth.

I live every day of my life attempting to do as Jesus did. I have compassion for others, choose love in all situations, and I try not to judge others. I feel that when we mimic the ways of Jesus, we are acting how our Creator wants us to act. Even if I am wrong here, love itself is a good feeling that everyone likes to be met with. Unfortunately, religion has provoked many wars and acts of terror. How is it that religion can cause such animosity when the foundation of most religions is love? In this chapter, I will try to make some sense of that, and show that regardless of what religion you are, we can all please God simply by being Love. This is part of why you are here.

Everyone has their own beliefs, and I firmly believe that we all need to accept that. There is a good reason why many people advise never to talk about religion or politics. I feel that is because most people are very passionate and deeply rooted in their beliefs when it comes to both.

After I started to learn more and more about life from all the books God led me to, I tried to share the information I learned with many of my friends. I tried to get them to understand that there is so much more to life and that there is a significant amount of enlightening information available. I wanted to help them understand what I discovered, so they could understand as well. I soon realized, after many uncomfortable conversations — and even some heated religious debates — that this is not something I want to engage in. I won't have debates about religion, and anyone can read what my personal beliefs are by reading this book or viewing them on my website. If someone has questions about what I have discovered, or wants to have a pragmatic, intellectual discussion about my beliefs, I will. However, if the person inquiring seems to come from anything but love or if the conversation gets uncomfortable, disrespectful, or heated, I will end the discussion.

There is something I would like you to consider since you are reading this book. Not everyone believes what you believe, and not everyone is the same religion as you. That does not mean they are wrong, and you are right, or vice versa. The sooner we respect other people's beliefs, the sooner we can make this world a better place. That applies not only to beliefs about religion or politics, but also to beliefs and opinions on everything. I am a big supporter of "to each their own." I think we all should support, love, and treat others with respect, regardless of their beliefs. Sit tight and continue reading with an open mind.

There are over two billion people on this Earth that claim to be Christian. There is no solid number as to how many denominations are within the world's largest religion. Since I was raised Catholic and have accepted Jesus into my heart, I speak from that perspective. I used to believe that we went to Heaven or hell *forever*. I used to believe that we only live one life, that the Bible is the absolute, perfect, only Word of God, that homosexuals were damned to hell, that Jesus is the *only* way to God, and that Jesus was the *only* Son of God.

If you believe those things, I still love you no matter what, and I don't judge you for your beliefs. You may be right, or you may be wrong. Just because I do not believe those things anymore, does not mean you should look at me, or anyone else who doesn't believe them, with anything but love. Even if you are an atheist, I love you with all my heart. No one on Earth truly knows the whole truth, so why not at least love each other unconditionally?

I would like to share my personal beliefs, along with what my religion of Love involves: I believe we should have compassion for every single human being under all circumstances, no matter what. I believe we should treat each other with respect, kindness, and love. I believe in God, and in Jesus, and I try to be like Him every single day. I believe that He is *my* way to God, but I *do not* believe that He is the *only* way. I do not think that He *has* to be *your* way to God.

In John 14:6, Jesus says, "I am the way, the truth, and the life. No one comes to the Father except through Me." (NKJV). Here, *I believe* Jesus is speaking about His teachings, not Himself. I personally choose Jesus, but I believe you can choose any route to God that you so desire.

If Jesus were the only way to God, according to some

peoples' interpretation of Scripture, the supporters of the other 4,000, or so, religions, comprised of approximately 5.5 billion people who don't believe Jesus was the only Son of God, could, again, by certain interpretations of the Bible, burn in hell eternally. I don't buy that. I believe that every single one of us is a son or daughter of God and we are all loved by Him *unconditionally*.

I read the Bible daily and thank God every day for His abundant amount of Love and for His blessings. I believe in reincarnation and different universes. I firmly believe that there is no way to fully know the truth about life and how it all works while we are in human form. My beliefs come from the many books I've read, including the Bible, and by having provided well over eight-hundred private mediumship readings, which include direct Spirit communication. I don't claim my beliefs to be absolute truth because there is no definitive way to know that they are. They are just what I believe based on all I have researched and experienced.

When I first "came out" as a medium, it was scary, uncomfortable, and risky. I knew people would look at me differently, and I also knew I would possibly lose some friends. Some people would think what I do isn't real, and others simply wouldn't understand it. The one thing, however, I never saw coming, was the degree to which mediumship was considered by some people to be against Christianity.

I will never forget when I received an e-mail from a former co-worker a few months after I came out as a medium.

Here I was serving God, helping others with grief, while spreading love and joy when, in a nice and caring way, this person told me I was channeling the devil and evil spirits, and that I was going to hell for it. I could tell from the tone of the e-mail and from what I knew of her, that she was coming from a place of good intention.

I must admit that my first reaction was, *Oh, no, I have to stop doing mediumship because I don't want to go to hell.* This was at an early stage in my research and readings, and I thought maybe there was something to what she said. So, I decided to investigate further, even though I had already spent well over a year preparing and doing copious amounts of research about the mediumship process. It felt so right to help others — especially grieving parents — in such a significant way and I was praying daily. I always protected myself with God's Light, but I was still concerned.

I started reading Scripture to see what it had to say about mediums, and, *oh, boy*, was I in trouble. Here are some Scriptures I found in the Bible about spirit communication. They will give you an idea of what the Bible says on the subject:

"There shall not be found among you *anyone* that maketh his son or his daughter to pass through the fire, *or* that useth divination, *or* an observer of times, or an enchanter, or a witch, or a charmer, or a consulter with familiar spirits, or a wizard, or a necromancer. For all that do these things are an abomination unto the LORD: and because of these abominations the LORD thy God doth drive them out from before thee." (Deuteronomy 18:10-12). (NKJV).

"And when they shall say unto you, Seek unto them that have familiar spirits, and unto wizards that peep, and that mutter: should not a people seek unto their God? for the living to the dead? To the law and to the testimony: if they speak not according to this word, *it is* because *there is* no light in them." (Isaiah 8:19-20). (NKJV).

"Regard not them that have familiar spirits, neither seek after wizards, to be defiled by them: I am the LORD your God." (Leviticus 19:31). (NKJV).

"And the soul that turneth after such as have familiar spirits, and after wizards, to go a whoring after them, I will even set my face against that soul, and will cut him off from among his people." (Leviticus 20:6). (NKJV).

"Moreover the workers with familiar spirits, and the wizards, and the images, and the idols, and all the abominations that were spied in the land of Judah and in Jerusalem, did Josiah put away, that he might perform the words of the law which were written in the book that Hilkiah the priest found in the house of the LORD." (2 Kings 23:24). (NKJV).

"Therefore, hearken not ye to your prophets, nor to your diviners, nor to your dreamers, nor to your enchanters, nor to your sorcerers, which speak unto you, saying, Ye shall not serve the king of Babylon." (Jeremiah 27:9). (NKJV).

"So Saul died for his transgression which he committed

against the LORD, even against the word of the LORD, which he kept not, and also for asking counsel of one that had a familiar spirit, to enquire of it; And enquired not of the LORD: therefore he slew him, and turned the kingdom unto David the son of Jesse." (1 Chronicles 10:13-14). (NKJV).

"And he made his son pass through the fire, and observed times, and used enchantments, and dealt with familiar spirits and wizards: he wrought much wickedness in the sight of the LORD, to provoke him to anger." (2 Kings 21:6). (NKJV).

"And he caused his children to pass through the fire in the valley of the son of Hinnom: also he observed times, and used enchantments, and used witchcraft, and dealt with a familiar spirit, and with wizards: he wrought much evil in the sight of the LORD, to provoke him to anger." (2 Chronicles 33:6). (NKJV).

"And the spirit of Egypt shall fail in the midst thereof; and I will destroy the counsel thereof: and they shall seek to the idols, and to the charmers, and to them that have familiar spirits, and to the wizards." (Isaiah 19:3). (NKJV).

I was extremely nervous after reading all these verses and thought maybe I had been fooled. *In all the readings I had done, which had significantly helped so many people in such a profound way, had the devil been fooling me? How could I have experienced all these synchronistic stories, amazing healings, and answers to my prayers, while being in a place of pure love if it was all a hoax?* I actually considered stopping my readings after viewing these passages from the Old Testament because the Bible has always been a guide for me throughout my entire life.

However, instead of quitting something my heart told me that God wanted me to do, I decided to take a step back and re-examine everything I have ever believed to be truth. I bought an audio version of the Bible and listened to all 40+ hours of it. I listened to the whole story from Genesis to Revelation. I continued to read Scripture daily and read many books about the Bible. I delved deeply into Biblical stories to help me understand the context and meaning behind what was written in Scripture. I was eager to do this, because I had always had some questions about the Bible and where it stood on sensitive topics like hell and homosexuality.

I had already come to believe that the Bible was not perfectly accurate and was open to individual interpretation. I didn't believe it was the infallible, complete truth. One of the main reasons was because I struggled with the concept of an eternal hell. *How could an all-loving God, who loves us unconditionally, send His children to hell forever just because they didn't believe in Jesus? Two-thirds of the world's population are not Christian, so are they all going to hell forever?* That was counterintuitive to what I believed about our Creator.

I am not saying that things need to make sense to be true. I just feel that sending your child to hell forever is not what an unconditionally loving God would do. Of all the religions in the world, why did Christianity have to be the "right" one?

The New Testament is approximately 2,000 years old and the Old Testament was written many years before that. It was written and transcribed by man and translated many times in many different languages. It was altered countless times by the Church throughout history. And because of this, I feel it is not perfect. I will say however, that I *love* the Bible. There are so many great Scriptures within the book, along with many great lessons and stories. I use the Bible and its content exclusively to spread God's Love and I feel we should all do the same. But I don't see every single verse as flawless and 100% applicable today. Many verses can easily be taken out of context.

The Bible is full of spirit communication and prophesy, even though the Old Testament can be interpreted in such a way that both these activities are discouraged or even considered demonic. Even Jesus was a prophet and a medium. (See John 4:19 and Matthew 17:3). That is one of the main contradictions in the Bible. I don't share these contradictions to discount the Bible. Not even a little. Again, it is a great book, with many good lessons and teachings. I do know people who read it literally as if it were 100% perfect, and in my opinion, that is not the best way to spread Love. For example, when your child does not obey you, it might not be the best idea to stone them to death. (Deuteronomy 21:18-21). When I first discovered what Old Testament verses said about mediumship, I was so confused. *How could this not be okay with God? And how could it be the "devil?"*

Throughout my mediumship journey, I had prayed every day, and God had given me so many miraculous signs along my path, that it's hard to put into words. After every single reading, each one of my sitters were so transformed in ways I can hardly explain. There was so much love, healing, and forgiveness. If this were "the devil" and "evil spirits," they were doing a hell of a job (pun intended), at helping people live better lives, and at the same time significantly improving each sitter's relationship with God.

I have had a plethora of e-mails and messages from my sitters after their readings, in which they explained to me how their lives had changed in profoundly positive ways. They could smile, knowing that their loved ones were okay, were still with them, and still had unconditional love for them. There had *never* been a reading in which an evil spirit had come in, and there had *never* been a message that did not come from a place of love. I had protected myself, as well as the sitter, in God's Light, and I did not deal with any energies that were not of His Light.

"Beloved, believe not every spirit, but try the spirits whether they are of God: because many false prophets are gone out into the world." (1 John 4:1). (NKJV).

Why would we need to try (test) the spirits if we are not to communicate with them? Think about that.

I had made a conscious effort to exclusively work with

energies that were in the "White Light of God." *After all the signs He gave me to do this work, how could this not be okay with Him?*

For the record, it is not very often that I get e-mails or messages in which people tell me I am going to hell or that what I'm doing is wrong. Ninety-nine percent of the messages and e-mails I receive, express ample amounts of love and support. I thank God and all of you for that. It is so heartwarming to know that God gave me a gift I can use to serve Him and help others.

Here is what I have to say, from a biblical standpoint, to show that God *does* support good-hearted mediums and that our gifts are *from Him*. I have investigated many of the verses quoted previously that denounce mediumship, and here are some major points to consider:

1. These Scriptures and laws, which are *all* in the Old Testament, are thousands of years old and simply do not universally apply today.
2. Jesus himself "disobeyed" some Old Testament laws and He was perfect and without sin.
3. Jesus was a prophet and a medium. Multiple Scriptures say we are to do as He does, *and more*, to help others.
4. One of Jesus' main messages was to show that eternal life exists and that we do not die. This is also one of the main objectives of most mediums.

If you look back at the "anti-mediumship" Scriptures that I've quoted, these books in the Bible often contain verses (laws), that simply do not apply today. Some of these books have verses that prohibit eating bloody meat (Leviticus 19:26), wearing shirts made from two types of materials (Deuteronomy 22:11), tattooing your body (Leviticus 19:28), or even shaving your face. (Leviticus 19:27). Deuteronomy 22:22 even demands that if a married man and a woman are caught being unfaithful, "they both shall die."

Back when books like Deuteronomy and Leviticus were written, things were vastly different. The people of that time were governed by the laws of the Sinai covenant. These rules were rules that were given to ancient Israelites. They were living in a very different time and culture than we live in today. When someone quotes these verses to me and says that I am going to hell or that I'm channeling the devil, they are most often coming from a place of fear, not love.

I hesitate to use the word "ignorant," when referring to people who send me an e-mail or message telling me I am doing the work of the devil, because that word is often not used properly. But they happen to be exactly that. They simply *do not know* about what *I* do or how so many people are profoundly helped by a mediumship reading. In many cases, they have not researched more than just one book — the Bible — which they actually contradict by judging me and sending me damning messages. (Matthew 7:1-5).

I want to note here that Scripture is still Scripture and it has its purpose and place in history. Even though some of its rules do not apply today in the same way they did back then, they *do* exist for a reason. Today, we have much more access to information and forms of protection from negative energies and spirits. The energy and conditions that existed in ancient Israel during the time and place when the Old Testament books were written, often made it unsafe to communicate with Spirit. Even after all the work Moses did, when he died, it seemed as if "the people of Israel had forsaken the Lord." (Deuteronomy 31:16). I believe that even now, in our current time, if you are *not* working for God to serve others, you *should not* practice mediumship. As I mentioned before, it is crucial when channeling Spirit, that you do it solely to serve God. I highly recommend that you *do not* engage in mediumship for any other reason than to spread His Love and do His work.

Another thing to consider, is that even Jesus did not "obey" some Old Testament Scripture. In John 8:3-11, Jesus defies Deuteronomy 22:22, by not killing, or even condemning, a woman for committing adultery. If Jesus, who is a true Christian's role model, *did not* follow some older Scriptures, then why should we blindly and unilaterally follow them 2,000 years later? Despite what Old Testament Scripture says, how can one damn or judge others when Jesus did not? How can we look at Scriptures that talk about mediumship and think they still apply today?

Not only did Jesus never once speak against mediums,

he was one. *Yes, Jesus was a medium.* In Matthew 17, Moses and Elijah, both deceased, appeared to Jesus and He spoke with them. This is "communication with familiar spirits," and happens to be the definition of a medium. When this occurred, Moses and Elijah had been "dead" for a very long time. The apostles, Peter, James, and John, were all with Jesus and witnessed this.

Here is the best part: Not only did Jesus communicate with the dead, but just two verses later, in Matthew 17:5, God announces how pleased He is with His son, right after Jesus "communicated with familiar spirits," which is, according to Deuteronomy 18, "detestable to the Lord." If communicating with the dead was truly detestable to God, why did He announce His pleasure with Jesus right after he did just that? *Think about that.*

Even with this evidence, some people will say to me, "Well, that was Jesus, He *is* God, and you surely are *not* Jesus." Of course, I'm not, and I don't claim to be Jesus. But some people seem to conveniently forget some New Testament Scripture about our role as followers of Him. John 14:12 says that "whoever believes in Jesus, will do the works He does and more." In 1 Corinthians 11:1, the apostle Paul encourages us to follow Jesus' example and do the works that He does. Corinthians 12:4-11 states that we are to use our gifts from God as we will, to help others, including "gifts of prophecy" and "discerning of spirits." More than any other, this passage from Corinthians is enough for me to know that I am serving God by using my gifts to help others.

My goal with each one of my sitters is to help them heal and to help them find, regain, or strengthen their faith in God. Spirit often comes through to pass on messages of a very specific nature, to let the sitters know that their deceased loved ones are still very present in their lives. I feel that by facilitating this communication, I am sharing the same message that Jesus did when He raised from the dead: *We do not die.*

I'm not comparing myself to Jesus as I am nowhere near His perfection. He did, however, teach us something about eternal life, especially when He was resurrected. When you come to a mediumship reading and receive messages from your loved ones, you know for certain they are still with you and that they still love you. They are somehow still involved in your life even though you cannot see them. This is beyond comforting. It can be life-altering.

I have completed a great deal of research on the concept of hell — the place a few people have told me I am going — and what the Bible says about it. Based on my readings and research, I believe that hell is perception and satan is ego. I don't believe in a "place" of eternal damnation after we die. Jesus did mention in John 14:2, that His Father's House has many mansions. I believe that after we die, we enter the afterlife at a certain vibration depending on our soul's karma and how we acted during our most recent life.

I used to think we live, die, then either go to Heaven or

are sent to hell forever. I no longer believe this at all. There is a significant amount of anecdotal evidence that reincarnation — which we will cover in the next chapter — exists, and that we live many lives in physical form. God created us as souls, and I believe that when we finally discover who and what God is while we are in physical form, we can escape the wheel of life and spend our real lives in bliss with God for eternity. Moses called it the "Promised Land." Buddha called it "Nirvana." Jesus called it "Heaven." I believe "It" is all the same thing, and *that* is eternal Love.

When we "lose" a loved one, it can be very depressing and debilitating. During the grieving process, one can often feel hopeless and lost in life because of the severity of the loss. Spirit uses people like me to guide other people toward enjoying life again and encouraging them to have stronger faith and, in turn, an improved relationship with God.

You do *not* need a medium to experience a connection to Source/Spirit. He is available to us all. Again, I am just here to help you find Him, and in turn, find your highest path.

Inspiration and communication from God/Spirit did not just suddenly stop 2,000 years ago. Many writings that are being penned today, and every single day, are inspired by God. Spirit communication also happens as much today as it did in Biblical times. God speaks to us in so many ways. In my opinion, the Bible is not the end-all-be-all. Change is constant and God is omnipresent.

We are all sparks of God, and as a whole, we make up

"all that is." God is everything. God is Love. He is our Creator, who we are, and what we come from. We are never separate; that is an illusion. We are all One. (John 14:20).

I hope this book wakes you up and that it also helps you acknowledge that God is the answer. He is the Way and the Truth. Trust in Him and know that He loves you unconditionally.

Here is the link to my video that discusses mediumship and its relationship to Christianity on my YouTube channel: https://www.youtube.com/DanielJohnMedium

Chapter 7
Reincarnation

Even before I discovered that I am medium, reincarnation was something I had always wondered about. I would say that I leaned significantly to the side of it *not* being real. *Boy, was I wrong on that one!*

As I was starting to go through my spiritual awakening — which is still very much ongoing — reincarnation was one of the first things I came to understand and believe to be true. I used to think it was impossible because it didn't seem to make sense. There is a *lot* of anecdotal evidence for things in this life that don't make sense to us as human beings, and reincarnation surely is one of them. At least to me anyway.

One day early in my awakening, I was online looking for books to educate myself, and a book randomly popped up in my "suggested books" called *Many Lives, Many Masters* by Brian Weiss. I added it to my watch list and moved on.

About a week later, I was driving through Geneseo, a small town in Upstate New York. I saw a quaint little bookstore and had a few extra minutes, so I figured I would check it out. As I walked in, I was greeted by a nice man who asked if I needed help finding anything. I said, "No, thank you," with a smile. Then I said a prayer. *God, please lead me to a book that can help me understand what You want me to know.* With Divine guidance, I went directly to a section in the bookstore, reached out my hand, and grabbed a book from the shelf. It was the same book I had seen in my suggestions list a week before! I could not believe it. If this wasn't a sign, I didn't know what was.

I purchased the book and started to read it immediately. It is one of the most fascinating books I have ever read. I highly recommend reading it, because it changed the way I look at life, and I believe it will do the same for you. It changed my worldview, and even though it was hard to comprehend at the time, my soul understood it to be truth.

Not only do most books I have read on the topic of spirituality, address reincarnation, they all also share it as truth. Even the Bible has verses that speak to reincarnation, such as Matthew 11: 13-15, Matthew 17:12-13, and John 3:3. There are many books, YouTube videos, documentaries, and other media sources, that all but prove reincarnation is absolute truth. It probably can't be proven unequivocally, but the reality of reincarnation being true is overwhelmingly supported.

I used to say to myself, *God made me as me. I could not be anyone else.* I feel that this is true and false at the same time. From the perspective of the soul, it is true because we are a spark of God's creation on our journey to enlightenment. From the human perspective, it is also true because our unique existence is also His creation. Why I feel it is false is because our bodies are just a vehicle for our soul as it journeys through many lives to enlightenment. I feel, based on all my mediumship readings, experiences, and studies, that we live many lives in physical form, in many different "times," to fulfill our soul's mission. I feel that our overall mission is to recognize, in material form, that we are all One and part of a greater Source of creation or God. I feel that we are all sparks of God, trying to find our way back to Him. You are yourself, as a soul, not only as a human being. Don't get me wrong, you are you, but there is a higher you, your soul, and that is your *true* self. *Make sense? Good!*

Things like past-life regressions, dreams of former lives, phobias and experiences carried over from other lives, in my opinion, are very real. I was given a past-life regression from someone who knew nothing about me, and it led me to an understanding of many things Spirit wanted me to know. This regression was very accurate and profound. I feel that when you understand reincarnation is truth, this knowledge shines a light on the way you live and changes your perceptive of life in profound ways. During my readings, I've had spirits share things with me such as, they had lived other lifetimes together with the sitter, or that they had already reincarnated in another body. On many occasions, they have even shared that they have been "soul mates" with the sitter throughout many lifetimes.

When you understand reincarnation and recognize that we are souls living a human experience, you will look at life through completely different lenses. As a soul, we are Love and nothing else. That is why we, as human beings, should approach every single situation in life with love. Love is who you are and what you are made of.

I am in no way suggesting that I know all the answers, and I cannot prove to you that reincarnation is real. The only thing I can do is to tell you that through everything I have experienced, I firmly believe it is true.

I want to stress that even though we live many lives in physical form, I feel that God is still the Creator of all. Every aspect of our lives is divinely guided and created by the Universe. As souls, we live many lives and we are uniquely created by God. Again, I highly recommend that you read *Many Lives, Many Masters* by Brian L. Weiss, M.D., because your understanding of who you truly are is so essential to your growth in this lifetime.

Consider having a past-life regression done for yourself as well if you feel compelled to do so. During a past-life regression, a therapist can bring you "into" your past lives to help you understand whatever it is from those lifetimes that can benefit you in your current life.

Former lives can help you understand your soul's mission, explain certain phobias, and help you address personality flaws and quirks, among other things. Open your mind and ask God if it is beneficial for you to experience a past-life regression. It is important to put past beliefs aside and trust in your heart, so you can learn what your soul craves.

Chapter 8
Angels and Spirit Guides

About a week before my first appointment with Beth —
the medium who changed my life forever — I had one of those
experiences I simply cannot explain.

I was in the shower and I kept sensing the name,
"Chuck." It was overwhelming and persistent. I remember
saying to myself, *Who are you, Chuck?* I thought I was nuts
for even thinking that.

A week later, about halfway through my appointment
with Beth, out of the blue she asked, "Who is Chuck?"

I couldn't believe it. *Out of tens of thousands of names,
why did she say that one?* Not only had I forgotten about the
experience in the shower, I hadn't told anyone about it. I told
Beth about what happened in the shower and explained that I
felt Chuck was my guardian angel or something like that. She
told me to trust that feeling. It was surreal for me at the time,
because it validated that the experience had been real,
especially since I was so skeptical about things like guardian
angels and receiving spirit messages.

Since I was at the beginning of my awakening process,
I had not yet conducted significant research or completed

much reading about the subject of metaphysics. After reading about what spirit guides are, I soon realized that Chuck *is* one of them. I knew he was there to protect me and guide me along my path here on Earth.

I believe we all have at least one spirit guide (or what most people call them, "guardian angels"), and many people have more than one. I know this sounds wild to some people, but it is important to know that these guides, who are souls/energies who have agreed to help us throughout this life, are here to support and help us any time we need them.

Certain guides specialize in different types of support. You can have the same spirit guide throughout one or many lifetimes. But as you evolve, you will often change spirit guides depending on your growth. The analogy to explain the change, is that you don't need a college professor if you are a kindergarten student. As you progress in your awakening, a more experienced guide, or guides, will assist you based on your needs.

Communication with your spirit guides is often *extremely* subtle. Guides often use imagery, symbols, synchronicity, and music, among many other ways, to connect with you. I also feel that there are restrictions to the quality and quantity of information they can provide to you. Communication will often depend on your life plan (your destiny), as well as your energetic vibration or frequency.

I would compare the subtlety of communication from spirit guides to be as "faint" as what I experience in my mediumship readings. This communication is usually *so* subtle that it feels as if you are making it up. Please know that even if you are "making it up," your subconscious mind is getting it from somewhere. So, there may very well be a significant amount of value in those feelings and thoughts. Trust is the biggest hurdle when receiving messages from Spirit.

While meditating one night, about one year into my awakening, I suddenly felt an energy around me. I asked in my mind, *Who are you?* The energy responded with, *I am George, your new spirit guide.* I must tell you that this dialogue felt 100% made up. I figured I had just fabricated it in my mind, and I dismissed it as such.

The next day, I was driving to Ithaca for work while listening to a podcast about soul paths. About twenty minutes into the program, the speaker started talking about spirit guides. I thought it was weird because of the experience I'd had during my meditation the night before.

As the guest continued to speak about spirit guides, I wondered if there was any possibility that what I experienced the night before had any truth to it. I kid you not, one second later, I saw a road sign that read "Gorges Street." I know that is not the same as "George," but it has almost the same letters (and that's how spirit communication works), and it happened at the exact moment I'd been thinking about my experience the night before.

Then, about three seconds after I saw that street sign, I saw another sign on the side of the road, advertising the play,

"It's a Wonderful Life." In that movie, which is my absolute favorite holiday classic — I literally watch it four or five times every Christmas season — the main character, George, meets his guardian angel/spirit guide. One could easily dismiss all this as coincidence. But because of where I am spiritually, I knew it was confirmation that my meditation experience was real. *Hey, George!*

It is comforting to know that along with God, we all have one, or many, guides we can lean on at any time while on our life journey. Remember to trust and know that your guide, or guides, are always available.

There is a hierarchy of angels and spirit guides that exists in the spiritual realm. I won't go into detail about that in this book, but from what I have learned, there are different levels of angels and guides. They are not on the sort of levels as people are here in this world. No one has authority over anyone else, but certain spirit guides are further along in their soul's growth.

Please know God has a "team" of energies that are available to help you. You can always ask for their guidance. Just remember to come from a place of love when you ask. Instead of asking to win the lottery or to win a game or contest, ask how you can best serve God and others. You will get back what you put out, whether it is in this life or the next.

It's as simple as "ask and you shall receive." (Matthew 7:7). Not only should your intention come from a place of love, but I feel you must build up a "love box" with good karma and good deeds in order to manifest what you desire. In other words, if you put a lot of positive energy into the world, you will get dividends in return. It is important to do good things with the intention of *not* getting anything back and do these things just for love.

I have such a blessed life. I feel the reason for this is because I have always come from a place of love. I want to let you know that you can live a blessed life too. We all can, as long as we lead with love-based decisions, thoughts, and actions. Abundance is available to every single one of us. The sooner we realize that, the better off the world will be.

Trust, have faith, and lean on God. Ask for His guidance and follow your heart (your soul), not your head (your ego). Serve Him and others, knowing that sometimes you may have to sacrifice something you value to appease God and/or to help others.

When I say I have led with love for most of my life, I mean it from the bottom of my heart. I look out for others, care about people, practice the Golden Rule, and help those in need. I thank God at least five to ten times a day for all He has provided for my family and for me. I encourage you to do the same, because being consciously grateful for all His blessings goes a very long way.

Be your own person, but please know that the Universe will take care of you when the foundation of all your thoughts, decisions, and actions, is pure love. You have a spiritual team ready, willing, and able to help you along your path.

Chapter 9
Pre-Life Planning

Would you be surprised if I told you that each one of us plans our life before we come to Earth? I feel that you are reading this book because your soul is looking for guidance, along with some answers about your plan.

By reading this book, you are sending an intention to the Universe that you would like to understand more about your life. You would like to understand why you are here. I assure you that your effort will not go unrewarded. I am a firm believer that everything is part of a bigger plan. You are supposed to be reading this, right here, right now. I was urged by my spirit guides to write this book for the purposes of helping you understand a little bit more about why you *are* here. As a medium, I have a unique perspective to share.

After completing a significant amount of research about spirit communication and near-death experiences, God led me to books with content that I wouldn't have believed before I began my spiritual journey. Two books by Robert Schwartz, *Your Soul's Plan* and *Your Soul's Gift,* changed my view of life. In these books, Schwartz's main concept is that we plan our lives before we incarnate here on Earth. As outlandish as that "theory" seemed as I read it, something in my soul "knew" it was the truth. I highly recommend reading these books, as they provide information that will change how you look at your life in significantly positive ways.

In the books by Schwartz, the overall premise is that we come to Earth to learn certain lessons to grow our souls. We plan each incarnation with our spirit guides, angels, and God. The purpose of our incarnations is for our souls to grow closer to Eternity, which, as previously mentioned, you can also refer to as "The Light," "God," "Bliss," "Enlightenment," "Nirvana," or the "Promised Land." Here in "Earth school," we balance karma, learn through opposites, experience limitations while in the physical body, and often experience difficult, "planned" events to fulfill our purpose.

It may sound crazy that all this planning could even be possible, but I firmly believe it to be true. The only way that you are likely to understand this is to read the books by Robert Schwartz. I would never have believed in any of this before because it goes against normal pragmatic thinking. Helping others to be open to things that sound unbelievable is part of my purpose in writing this book.

Another thing Schwartz addresses in his books is that we have made decisions before we incarnated, to meet certain people, experience pain, and to play specific roles — even "bad" ones. From what I understand, there is a web of possibilities during each of our incarnations.

God has blessed us all with free will to make our own

decisions while we are here, and as souls, I feel that is part of the challenge. Even if there is a situation where the "worst" thing happens, it is up to us to react with love. Some major things happen in our lives — some things that don't make sense, and some that are so painful both physically and/or mentally — that they seem unbearable. It is fascinating to know that all our possible life experiences are actually part of our own design. Whether it is a disease, the loss of a loved one, or even our own "premature" death, it is all part of a bigger plan, and something our souls designed during the planning stages of our lives, prior to arriving here on Earth.

When I first read about life plans, one of the biggest questions I had concerned the duality of free will and destiny. I was under the impression they are opposites. *How can free will exist, while at the same time, some things are just "meant" to happen?* This is one of those concepts that is hard to understand from our human perspective. I have watched some podcasts given by Robert Schwartz and he explains it this way: Think of a video game. The designer of the game programs the parameters of possibilities into the game. On the screen, you may be able to jump, run, or walk, but you can only engage in the specific activities that were initially programmed into the game. For example, if you are playing the video game Super Mario Brothers™, you can only jump so high or run so fast. You can only go down certain tubes/paths. This analogy helped me understand the duality of free will and destiny, and how it applies to our lives.

We can create and experience life in many ways and we all have the free will to live the way we want. Certain things have a high probability of happening based on the pre-life plan we have orchestrated for ourselves. While we are here, we can navigate our experiences the way we choose. The overall concept is that with free will, certain roads can take us down alternative, pre-destined paths that our soul agreed to navigate in this lifetime. The possibilities and options are many, but they are within the parameters of our pre-life plan's outline.

Striving for further understanding, one day while in my kitchen, I asked my spirit guides a question: "How do free will and destiny co-exist?" I asked. The answer I received was so profound, I knew it couldn't have come from me.

They said, "The major points along your life path will remain the same, but the roads you take to get there will differ." That makes total sense to me, and I couldn't have come up with that without spiritual guidance.

Your life can take many different paths, but it is so important to remember that the possibilities are vast, and they are predetermined, in soul form, by you. If you "lose" a loved one, break a bone, get a divorce, catch a cold, or someone chooses not to be friends with you anymore, it is all part of a grander plan. So, it is in your best interest to trust and accept everything that presents itself in your reality. When you understand and practice this acceptance, it is easier to choose love, forgiveness, and compassion, when confronted with some of life's most difficult situations. Please remember, that any experience you have is something that your soul agreed would be a possible outcome in this lifetime. Think about that and be at peace with every single thing that happens in your life.

Chapter 10
The Law of Attraction

The Law of Attraction is the number one law of the Universe. The main principle of this law is that "like attracts like." In other words, what we put out into the world through our thoughts and actions, creates our reality. When you fully grasp this major aspect of your life, it can lead you to downright abundance. I firmly believe that every single person in this world can experience life to its fullest, regardless of their situation. I will give you some examples, but what I want you to understand when reading this chapter is that you really can create your own experience. The number of opportunities and experiences you can enjoy are vast. All it takes for you to experience abundance is to be aware, be positive, and be Love.

One of the most influential books I have ever read is *The Law of Attraction* by Jerry and Esther Hicks. This book explains how you can pretty much create anything you wish with the right amount of energy and the best of intentions. You can create things, whether they are "positive" or "negative," by focusing your attention on them. This law allows us, as human beings, to use our God-given gift of free will to create what we desire within our own personal reality. It gives us the power to create the life we desire and helps guide us to our highest path. I feel that understanding the Law of Attraction is essential to our success as human beings. Please know that you have the ability to create your life. Use your free will along with the power of the Law of Attraction to create the life that you love.

In 2018, I started a new job as a sales rep for a pharmaceutical company. It was during this time that I was reading many books that discussed the Law of Attraction. From the time I started this new job, I stated my intention and set my goal to be the number one sales rep in the entire company. Every day, and sometimes multiple times throughout each day, I said aloud, "I *am* the number one rep in this company." As uncomfortable as it was to do, I even updated my resume halfway through the year with this designation. After setting and repeating my intention and goals daily, along with working hard to achieve them, I finished as the number one rep in the entire company for 2018. *Number 1!* I saw this as a test to see if the Law of Attraction would work. And it did. Try it for yourself.

Come from the heart with all your thoughts, while you set your intentions, and the Universe will align so your intentions can become reality — if it's a possibility in your life plan. It is important to trust, have faith, and come from a place of pure love when you do this. It is always good to add the phrase, "with harm to no one" as well, when setting your desired intentions. I have heard crazy stories about people praying and meditating so hard for things to happen, that they actually manifested whatever it was, but with a significant cost. Just be pure in your intentions and let the Universe know that you are asking with love.

I don't quite understand what the limitations are to the Law of Attraction, but I assume there are some. I feel that it is best to use this law to help others, while also using it to your advantage. Ultimately, it is up to you how you decide to use your God-given gift of free will.

Darek, a good friend of mine, is someone who understands and uses the Law of Attraction very well. He not only uses this law to make life better for himself and his family, but he also uses it to infuse positivity into the world and directly to the people he interacts with. From the time I met him, Darek has always been one to put other people first. He is even better at it than I am, and I put others first all the time. He is one of the most selfless people I have ever met. Our friends always joke and say, "God loves Darek and Dan," because things always seem to work out for us. I think this is partly because we lead with love and put others first, but it is also because we always see the best in every situation, even if it is not "good" or "ideal."

With love, Darek and I do our best to create what we desire, but when things don't turn out how we wanted them to, we understand that God had a different plan. I feel like the combination of perspective and intention, along with our gift of free will, and our acceptance of destiny, is what creates our own reality. It is best to seek and understand the positives that come from every situation we, as human beings, experience.

I cannot stress enough that the Law of Attraction is real, and it is something you can use to your benefit every single day. When you wake up in the morning, take a minute or more to thank God for your life. Set your goals and desires and love the fact that you are blessed with another day in which you have the opportunity to enjoy this beautiful Earth. Your soul and the Universe will benefit exponentially. Just by choosing love, and expressing gratitude, your path will be illuminated, and abundance and joy will work its way into your reality.

I must mention again that being thankful for what you have goes such a long way. Letting the Universe know you are appreciative of what It has provided you, pays significant dividends. It is like a domino effect. When you spread love, express thankfulness, and treat others with respect and love, life has the potential to be absolutely amazing. Then, if a little bump, or even a big bump, disrupts your journey, you can accept that it is Divine, and recognize the opportunity within the disruption. If you ask God to help you see the good in things, He surely will. When you are on your highest path, even the big "negative" things — like the death of a loved one, a disease, or even defamation — cannot bring you down. You will just understand that whatever is happening is part of the "Grand Design." Remain positive, spread love, and be thankful. This perspective will change your life.

I want to end this chapter by highlighting the single most important thing in life, no matter what happens to you along your path. *Love!* I know I have not said it much, but love is the *only* thing that truly matters both in and out of this world. If you lead with love at all times, you will experience your best life, and your connection to Source will become more obvious. When you leave this world, all you will have is what is left in your heart.

There are going to be situations in your life in which your ego will make it challenging to lead with love. There will be times when choosing to lead with love can feel almost impossible given the situation. Choosing love is all part of the process, and learning to make that choice, is one of the main reasons you are here. By leading with love as often as you can, you will operate at your highest vibration and you will exude positive energy. People will want to be around you. You will make them smile and you will attract positivity.

Chapter 11
Forgiveness

Spirit has continuously demonstrated that a lack of forgiveness is something that can have a significantly negative effect on your energy and on your quality of life. There is a very good possibility that you know someone who has done something "wrong" to you or to someone you know. Sometimes these things are minor and other times someone has done something that *seems* unforgivable. This chapter is all about letting those things go, no matter how "bad" they are. Having these feelings of resentment, bitterness, and animosity toward another person, is not only not love, it is extremely damaging for all the parties involved, especially you.

I am not denying the existence of situations that can cause significant amounts of pain. I am just saying that things are going to happen; people will make mistakes, and some people just don't get it. It is always in your best interest to let these things go and forgive those who committed whatever they did, no matter the severity of the action. It will be a huge benefit to you if you choose to forgive, even when someone else's actions caused severe pain to you or to someone you love.

When I say to "let go" of offenses, I do *not* mean that you should forget them. I do mean, however, that if there is a discussion that needs to happen, you should have it. If there is an e-mail you could write or a phone call you could make to put that forgiveness into action, write it or make that call. Bad feelings and negative energy do not just go away. Sometimes they need to be addressed, and other times, depending on the situation, they can just be forgiven internally with no action.

Use your judgment, but please make sure that you don't bury your feelings, because when you do, those feelings do not disappear. They can easily resurface at any point throughout your life. Be your own judge and decide whether the forgiveness needs to be actively addressed, or whether the offense can just be tacitly forgiven (not necessarily forgotten). Ask yourself how you can transform a situation into something higher. Ask God or your spirit guides for help. I will give you some examples from my own personal experience that will hopefully help you understand the difference.

Even though I was voted "most friendly" in our senior class of over six-hundred people, I would often hold grudges for the littlest things. Through my spiritual awakening, I quickly discovered that these negative feelings I had been holding onto, were not good for anyone, especially me. I would even hold grudges against people who hurt others, even when it didn't involve me, simply because I judged them. I could give you many examples of how I held grudges, from smallest gravity to the immensely serious, and it was not healthy. We

should all take advice from Princess Elsa from the Disney®
movie, *Frozen*, and just, "Let it go!"

Here is my proposal to you: I want you to consider
forgiving everyone for *everything. Can you do it?* If you do,
you will feel amazing and it will raise your vibration.

About one year into my enlightenment, I made a list of
every single person I held a grudge against. There were not
too many, but there were enough to make a list. It turned out
that the list included three acquaintances (former friends), two
family members, and a handful of random people, like
contractors. As hard as it was, I reached out to most of those
people via e-mail and apologized to them for the things that
had happened between us, even if I thought I had no fault in
the situation. Remember, it takes two to tango. I also forgave
them 100%. It was not easy, as some of the people on the list
had hurt me severely and never apologized for it. I did it all the
same.

As difficult as it was to do, it was so freeing, and I felt
so good afterward. A couple of people did not respond to me,
but most of them wrote me back and cleared the air. There
were also a few people on the list that I decided not to contact.
For those few people, I just chose to forgive them internally
and let go of the grudge. One of them was someone who
owed me $300 and never paid me. Every time I saw this
person, I would give them a dirty look. Now when I see them, I
smile at them and I don't even think about the money anymore
(*Well. . .I still do think about it, but I have no negative feelings*

toward them, just love). That was the end of me holding grudges toward anyone, and I highly encourage you to do the same, regardless of the severity of their "offense."

Forgiveness Party Exercise (Please do not skip this):

Make a list with three columns. In the first column, put the name of the person, or even the situation, that needs forgiving. In the second column put the details about the situation and why you feel the way you do about them/it. Lastly, in the third column, put the action you plan on taking to accomplish the forgiveness. Read through each item on the list individually. Please do not rush through this. Some of the actions in column three may take a significant amount of time and effort to complete. Once you have actively forgiven the person/people or situations on the list, you can consider yourself grudge-free. Your life will never be the same. Remember that you don't always have to contact a person directly or actively address the situation you have on the list in order to resolve it. There may be a person on the list who has passed away or who might be unreachable. That does not mean there may not be a significant forgiveness opportunity.

I gave a reading last week where the sitter's mom was actually mad at her husband for dying. That feeling of resentment toward her husband may have been a forgiveness opportunity for her, even though he is deceased. Believe it or not, forgiveness can actually help a person/energy in spirit as well. It is important to remember that we do not die, and our soul lives on forever. Forgiving those in spirit will help them energetically.

Grudges against others can significantly lower your vibration. Whether your resentment is toward a stranger who cuts you off on the road, or a friend stabs you in the back — figuratively, or even literally — it is in your best interest to forgive them. I know that last one sounds a little extreme but let me share a story with you that I find truly inspiring. Reading it will help you initiate your own "forgiveness party."

I read a story of a woman whose daughter was killed by a drunk driver. The driver was sentenced to twenty-two years in jail. A few years later however, the mom asked for the driver's sentence to be cut in half because she forgave him. The judge agreed, on the principle that forgiveness was a better option than any other. The mother and this man then traveled across the country to speak to students as co-advocates against drunk driving. You can read the full article here: https://www.littlethings.com/meagan-forgives-eric

The mom, Meagan, said she could hate him forever, but that it wouldn't do either of them any good. She went on to mention that forgiveness is the only way to heal.

I use this story as an example, because I feel if this woman can forgive the man who killed her own daughter, we can all forgive anyone for absolutely anything.

Certain things can happen in our lives that give us the opportunity to choose love over fear. When it comes to forgiveness, it can be quite difficult to choose love when someone does something to you or someone you care about. You could be angry, hurt, or even devastated. I ask you to simply consider forgiving all who have "wronged" you. Whether what they did was a free will choice or whether it was part of a pre-life plan, it is up to you to forgive. There will even be times when it is in your best interest to forgive, even when the person doesn't ask for it, and/or you may not think they deserve it. Don't let *anything* stop you from giving them love and letting go of any resentment toward them for what they did.

Remember, we can hold negative feelings for people even when they did not wrong us specifically, but instead, they did something to someone we know, or possibly someone we don't know. So, when you see a person on the news who did something "wrong," please send them compassion and forgiveness rather than hatred and disgust, because all they really need is love. The less we absorb negative energy, the easier we can live on our highest path. Just being conscious of these negative thoughts and emotions is a good place to start. Let past, current, and future negative emotions toward others go, and you will be on your highest road.

The last thing I want to mention in this chapter is I recommend that you do not believe everything you hear. Unfortunately, some people lie, spread rumors, and like to gossip. Please do me a favor, and when you hear something from someone — especially when it has a negative attachment to it — *don't assume it is truth.* People have opinions, and some lives have been ruined via rumors and untrue gossip. Don't believe everything you hear. I also recommend that you don't say *anything* that could be taken negatively, *ever,* especially when it is something negative about someone else. Don't assume! And keep it positive all the time.

Chapter 12
Love Will Find the Way

I firmly believe that everything in this world has a foundation of either love or fear. I know I have not said it much so far in this book, but when you have a thought, make a decision, choose a perspective, or perform an action, let it be from a place of love. When you lead with love instead of fear, you slowly make the world a better place. This sounds so simple, and I believe it is. As you now know, leading from a place of love consistently is my personal goal, and I encourage you to make it yours if you haven't already. It is not always easy, but it will raise your vibration and help you live on your highest path.

There is genuinely *nothing* to fear. I don't like to use clichés, but President Roosevelt (FDR), was onto something when he said, "The only thing to fear is fear itself." When you understand there is more to this world than what we can comprehend as human beings, and you trust that God has a perfect plan, you will accept that everything that happens is a part of a very well organized "Grand Design." I feel that is what is meant by Proverbs 3:5-6, where it says, "Trust in the LORD with all your heart; and lean not on your own understanding. In all your ways submit to Him, and he will make your paths straight." (NKJV).

When something happens in our lives that appears to be "negative," it may not truly be so. And even though we may view something as "negative," it is *always* part of God's plan. He knows better than we do about how things will influence our lives and how they will affect the world.

For example, I remember when my college girlfriend of two years broke up with me. I was devastated. Even though I was hurt, and it seemed tragic at the time, that breakup enabled me to experience a whole new life. And even though I didn't understand why it happened at the time, I trusted that God had something in mind that would lead me, and her, to a path that He wanted. We are now both happily married to our soul mates, have our own kids, and we even keep in touch to this day.

I'm not saying that we are just supposed to sit around and wait for things to happen because everything is governed by destiny anyway. I simply mean that when something happens that we do not like or understand, trust and accept that God knows what is best for us and for the world. It may be a car accident, a breakup, or even a disease, but please trust that He knows what He is doing. Take every moment in your life to drop fear and choose love. I am confident that doing so will lead you to your highest path.

Here is an example: While driving home from the

airport after a week-long business trip, I ran out of gas two miles from my exit. I was annoyed because the gas gauge indicated I still had forty miles worth of gas left in the tank. I was tired, it was cold, and I had not seen my wife and kids in five days. There I was on the side of the road, and I could have gotten very upset. Instead, I asked, *God, why did this happen?* I then experienced the same type of communication I did while raking the leaves in 2012: *You ran out of gas now because the tank's mileage estimate is not correct. It could have been a lot worse if it happened at another time. This was to protect you and to prevent you from trusting that gauge.*

I don't know who or what gave me that thought, but I called the tow truck and sat there for well over an hour just appreciating life and feeling thankful to be alive. I got home safely and didn't think about it much after that. I could have put a negative post about that experience on social media and spread the anger/fear. I could have let that situation ruin my day, my night, or even my week. But instead, I chose a "love perspective." I accepted what had happened and moved on with a smile.

When you're vibrating at a high level, and start to see love and not fear, you can look at every situation, including "negative" ones, in a different light. I know that running out of gas is not life-threatening, but it is just one example of how one can take a "bad" situation and trust that it is part of something that will lead to a higher path, even if it seems inconvenient at the time.

Everything that happens in your life can be looked at from different perspectives. When you look at everything primarily from a "love perspective," life can be very fulfilling. To me, it is fulfilling because when we do, we are serving God with all our actions. I choose Love every day because that is who and what I believe God is. John 4:8 tells us, "He that loveth not knoweth not God; for God is Love." (NKJV).

Whether it is someone who cuts me off while driving, gives me a dirty look, or sends me a message telling me I'm going to hell for the work I do as a medium, I send the person as much love as possible. Believe me, it is not easy sometimes, but I do the best I can to send everyone love, *no matter what*.

I cannot express enough that if you live your life with love, kindness, compassion, forgiveness, appreciation, and respect for our Source, you will operate at a high vibration, which is good for you and everyone around you. "Bad" things will still happen, people will pass away, and you will still have many challenges. Instead of reacting to those situations with fear, respond with love.

Another example I would like to share from my own experience was when we had a contractor perform some major renovations on our house. This contractor left nails in the driveway, charged me significantly more than he had estimated, did not provide receipts, and he was extremely disrespectful, sarcastic, and rude. When he sent me the final bill and I called him to ask for an explanation — because it

was thousands of dollars more than he had said it would be —
he yelled at me and threatened to take me to court. I looked at
the phone, amazed. I was shocked he was acting like this.

I paid the bill and then I wrote him an e-mail out of pure
love. I didn't threaten him, belittle him, or even get mad at him.
I took the high road and it felt so good. Here is what I wrote. I
changed some small details and names for privacy purposes:

Joe,

Your check is in the mail.

*As you read this e-mail, you can probably see that
there is a lot of writing below. It is obviously up to you
whether you read it or not, but I hope you do. Know that my
intention in this e-mail is to help you. It is not to berate or
harm in any way, but just to help.*

First, I want to apologize to you.

*After we got off the phone last night, I thought to
myself, "What did I do wrong here?" I am sorry for making you
feel uncomfortable every time you gave me a bill. It was not
fair or nice of me to make comments like" Wow" or "Really?"
That can't feel good, to provide a service to someone and
have them act like that. I am very sorry for that. You have
taught me a lesson there.*

*Second, I would like to say, the remodel does look
great and the people you have working for you are stand-up
guys. The precision work and most of the detail work looks
great!*

The garbage in the garage and the windows on the

back porch. . .would have been nice if you disposed of that, but maybe that's not something you normally do. Everything looks good, and then there is this junk left behind. I don't get that, but that is just some feedback. But overall, it looks great! Thank you for that.

Lastly, I don't like that things ended the way they did. I can't imagine that you did.

You shared some things with me about your life that I would not have known. . . It would be unfair for me to say that I understand, or that I know how you feel, because I don't. There is no way I could.

From what you have told me, you have met some major challenges (and you don't lead me to believe that you told me to "feel bad for yourself" or ask for sympathy). You have raised children, have a wife, and have a successful business. You must be proud of that. Not many people have the power and ability to overcome even one of those challenges. You should be proud of yourself! Really!

Without getting into too many details, it was unfortunate to have a phone conversation like that, when all I wanted was to have some receipts so I could warranty my products. Then you had to threaten court and say things like "It's not my problem," and "They were your people." I did reread the e-mail and can see why you read it that way. It was because you told me the final bill would be in the hundreds, and it was over $3,000. Any normal person would like an explanation for that. Even if you did read into the e-mail, I instantly texted you to stop by next week so we could talk about it and you never wrote back.

I just flew home last night, sent you a follow-up text to stop over, and then received your phone call. You were aggressive, rude, unkind, assumptive, and patronizing. Then, calling you afterward to reason with you and you saying I interrupted your dinner. . . I don't even know what to say. How am I supposed to know you were eating dinner? Don't answer the phone next time! I was just trying one more time to reason with you, even though you were quite unreasonable. That was not fair to treat someone like that under ANY circumstances. That was simply not nice. Telling Mark that I don't pay you when I clearly do, me sending you a simple text with a question, and you acting like you did (making me feel uncomfortable for texting a simple question. . .there is no way I could have known that you were in bed at 7:30), was just mean! Then saying things behind my back to multiple people, is simply not nice.

It may be hard to see, but this e-mail is intended to help you accomplish why you are here on this Earth. The cards you were dealt in this life were given for to you for a reason. The challenges you have are there for a reason. Please choose love when you deal with people. I have found that when I lead with love instead of anything else, things turn out way better.

Again, there is no way to know how you feel. I do know, however, that you said verbatim, "I don't want to be here on Earth." You are here for a reason. Anytime you have the chance to interact with people throughout the rest of your time here, please be nicer. It will only help you and your soul. I asked myself what I could have done differently during this process and I apologized for it in this e-mail. I encourage you to do the same.

I don't want an apology or even a response from you. I would prefer that you don't, unless you find this e-mail hits home for you. My desire for you is to lead the best life you can while you are here and treat others with respect and love.

I have written this knowing there is a high probability that you will not read this and/or take it the wrong way. I was willing to take that risk to help another soul in their life here.

Joe, I see a glimmer of light in your eyes when I talk to you. I know that your soul wants and needs this life to grow closer to God. This is your chance to right the wrongs and lead with love.

I hope you do. Much love to you, Joe.

Daniel

This contractor never wrote me back, but I have completely forgiven him for the way he acted and for how he treated our family. I don't want to make it sound like I am perfect and react perfectly in every situation, because I'm not, and I don't. However, I did want to give you an example of a situation that could have gone down a lot worse had I chosen not to take the higher road.

Please remember, that in most, if not all cases, you do not know what other people are going through. Someone who was rude to you while in line at the grocery store may be going through a very rough time. Maybe they just lost their job. Maybe they had a house fire. There is a possibility that they just lost a loved one or even had a child pass away. You just don't know, and since you don't know, choose to be kind to them even though they may have been rude to you.

I stopped watching the news a few years ago, because as I've mentioned, we are energy, and we can easily be influenced by others' actions, words, thoughts, and feelings. I encourage you to watch the news one evening, and then on a piece of paper make two columns. Write, "This makes me feel good," at the top of one column. And write, "This makes me feel not so good," at the top of the other. You will undoubtedly find that one column has significantly more entries than the other. When we see things that give us "negative" feelings, our energy is negatively affected. Watching such negative newscasts day after day can have a major effect on our perspectives and our auras.

Consider eliminating news-watching from your daily activity. I strongly feel that news programs would be a better experience for the viewer if more "feel-good" stories were added. Celebrating positivity and goodness is something that should flood the daily news. It would help society to see that there is a lot of good happening in this world.

I mentioned this in the previous chapter, but I want to revisit it, so it sinks in: When you see or hear something negative, like one of those news stories, or even a friend or family member talking negatively about someone else. . .send love! Don't judge, don't believe everything you hear, and give people the benefit of the doubt. One of the things I noticed as I started to spiritually awaken, is all the "shit" people talk about each other. During those conversations, negativity can easily become the default mode. Therefore, if you hear someone talking negatively, send love to every part of the conversation. Send it to the person speaking, the person they are speaking negatively about, and to all involved. I used to sit and think, *Man, that person should not be talking shit about that other person. They are not being nice.* Now I simply send as much love as I can to the person talking negatively, because they need love as well.

If you find yourself saying, thinking, or feeling something that is not of love, I encourage you to acknowledge it. And then stop it. Remember, just being aware of these fear-based feelings is the first step. Let love flow from your mouth, through your thoughts, and within your actions. As you awaken spiritually, you will see that some people are just not aware. So just send them love. People will continue to speak without knowing they are coming from a place of fear, not love. Be the voice, image, and energy of love. Ask yourself in everything you do, think, or say, *Is this love?*

I don't know why, but throughout my life, I have always asked God if my actions were aligned with His plan. I feel that we are part of Him, and we are to honor and respect Him. This conscious "permission" from Him, leads you to your best life. As I mentioned before, I have a non-traditional view of God, in that I feel that God, the Universe, Source, and Allah, are all the same. I feel that God is beyond our understanding and language. I don't believe that God is a guy in the sky with a staff and a rod. The best way I can describe God with our inadequate words, is to say that He is an all-knowing, unconditionally loving, all-encompassing Source of all that is. We are each just one little spark of His energy and all our ideas of separateness from the One that is Him, are an illusion. Everything that exists is connected, and that connected whole is God.

I cannot emphasize enough that prayers do work, and their effectiveness is undeniable. Any thought you have is a creation. I feel that meditation and prayer go hand in hand, so I do include prayers to God in my meditations. I ask Him for protection and ask that His Love be present through all my mediumship readings and with everyone involved in them. Prayers are just a form of thoughts with intention. Whether it is to a friend, your late father, or to the big guy Himself, praying is something I encourage you to do daily. Why wouldn't you take thoughts of love and send them out? It is not about saying the perfect prayer or memorizing one and saying it without fault. It's always about your intention.

Regardless of what you believe about God, and what words you use to describe Him or "It," choosing to look at life from a perspective of love will help you be the best you that you can be. Every day, we are given opportunities to choose love over fear. Ask Him how you can make the best out of any situation. Ask Him for guidance as you make your daily decisions and actions. Believe me, He will guide you in so many ways. His guidance can be relayed to you from another person, through song lyrics, within the words of a book, or sometimes through a subtle, internal thought. Trust that guidance and trust your intuition. Be aware of what the Universe is trying to tell you.

Choose love, always. I promise you it always wins. When you consciously decide something based entirely out of love, then even if a situation turns out to be "unfavorable," the outcome is most likely a blessing in disguise. Garth Brooks was onto something when he wrote, "Unanswered Prayers." Listen to the lyrics of that song. They are powerful. Trust and surrender.

Chapter 13
Don't You Go Dyin' On Me

Death is not the end. There is so much more to life that I want to share with you. There is absolutely *nothing* to fear. What I have learned about death from my experience as a medium, and from the extensive research I've done on near-death experiences, has led me to an understanding that is vastly different from what I used to believe.

When we pass on, it is simply our time to leave this Earth. The physical bodies we use to experience life on Earth, before our transition back Home to Spirit, are only temporary, as are all the material things in this world. Your body is the vehicle in which your soul chose to experience this lifetime. Once your body is gone, you still exist, as Jesus proved through His teachings and His resurrection.

One of the most prevalent messages Spirit delivers during many of my readings is that when it is your time to leave your present life, it is simply your time to go. The people left behind won't miss their loved ones any less by knowing this. But this information can take the edge off a grieving person's pain to know that the circumstances behind a loved one who passed, were chosen by their soul. I have had an overwhelming number of spirits who have confirmed that their death was predetermined. Spirit has confirmed many times that every single one of us has our own specific window, or windows of time, in which we are meant to leave this Earth. It is ultimately up to the soul, with direction from God, as to how our transition back Home will occur, but it is 100% part of our destiny. There are *no* accidents. *None.*

I have given many readings to parents who have lost children, and it seems that almost all of them had a "feeling" that something "like this" would happen well before it did. The spirit of the deceased child usually shares this information with me well before the parents *do* confirm that they did indeed have this feeling prior to the child passing. The soul will share this information to confirm that their parent knew, on a soul level, that the child was meant to incarnate and leave "early" for some greater cause.

Through my readings, I have witnessed some of the most amazing reunions with parents and their deceased children. If you experienced even a fraction of these reunions, you would be in complete awe. When we love someone, and they pass away, there is often the question of, "Why?" Please know that *all* transitions back Home, are part of a "Grand Design."

While in my freshman year at college, I met a beautiful girl named Katie. She was pretty, super nice, and very down-to-earth. Okay, I'll admit I had a little crush on her. The night I met her, she told me the story of how a few of her best friends were murdered a couple of years prior, and she was supposed to be with them the morning they were killed. She had "randomly" decided not to meet up with them that fateful day. As I spoke to her, I could see she had survivor's guilt, but at the same time, she was so grateful to be alive. I remember feeling honored to have met her because she was such a kind person and she very well might not have been with me that evening.

We spoke a few times on the phone that year before each of us went back home for the summer. As I returned to the dorms for my sophomore year, I saw a flyer on the ground outside my building, sharing information about a candle-lighting ceremony that evening. It stated that the ceremony was being held that evening for a student who had passed away two months earlier. *It was Katie.*

Katie had died in a car accident in June that summer. I couldn't believe it! I felt so bad for her and her family, but I firmly believe that Katie passed away within the window of time she was meant to pass. She also may have chosen — before she incarnated — to survive one situation, and instead, leave her earthly body in another. Either way, I am confident that it was her time to go. I do not doubt that her passing has led to countless positive effects within her community and around the world, most of which I'm sure we cannot even begin to fully comprehend.

Have you ever read one of the many stories about someone who missed their flight and then it crashed? Have you heard about that person who didn't get into a car one night because they had a bad feeling and there ended up being a fatal accident? Those things are not coincidence. They all happen for a reason that most often we can't understand. Please know that when someone passes away and returns to their true Home in the spirit world, it was simply their time to leave their physical body.

I often have the honor of communicating with the soul of a person who has committed suicide. It is often the case that the friends and relatives of the deceased person have many regrets about not having been able to prevent the suicide. And since the sitter often has a significant amount of guilt about the situation, the information I pass on to them can be extremely comforting and healing.

Every reading is different, but the overwhelming theme in suicide cases is that the person who committed the act, is okay, and they are still with their loved ones energetically. Sometimes there is regret on the part of the person who was responsible for their own death, but sometimes there isn't. They are definitely not in "hell," although sometimes they admit to me that they must work on things at a lower vibration, in spirit, before they can incarnate again.

I once had a soul communicate to me that their suicide was a way out of that life for them and they didn't regret their choice to follow through with it. It was uncomfortable to hear, to be honest, but that particular spirit did tell the sitter they were sorry for the way the passing made them feel, even though they didn't regret the action.

If you are a grieving person, and you are having a hard time, I encourage you to pray and ask God for guidance. I do what I do because some people have lost their faith in Him. They are so caught up in grief that their energy is blocked. I have had spirits tell me they have tried to contact the sitter, but the spirit cannot reach them because of the blockage. This is where meditation and prayers come in.

Because our loved ones can communicate with us in our dreams, remember to pay attention to them. During sleep, we enter certain brain-wave activities that enable us to be more receptive to messages from the spirit realms. If you dream of a loved one, pay attention, and trust it really is them. Most dreams of loved ones are them actually communicating with you. If you have a bad dream about a loved one, on the other hand, it is unlikely to be your loved one in spirit. Bad dreams are usually a sign that your heart is healing in some way. It may seem strange that bad dreams are for healing, but I feel very confident that is the case.

Some signs that validate that a loved one is actually visiting you in your dream, are that the dream is very vivid, they communicate something to you with thoughts, not words, or they just hug you. Use your intuition to connect with and dream of your loved ones who have passed. They *will* come to you if they are supposed to do so. Occasionally, I have such vivid dreams of my dad that I don't even realize I am dreaming. We just hang out and hug. These dreams are wonderful because I do miss him. You can experience the same if the time and intentions are right. Ask, and be patient.

If you would like to contact a loved one in spirit, please seek God before you reach out to a medium. I cannot say enough, that in my opinion, you do not need a medium, but you do need God. We all can connect with our loved ones in spirit, but some people need a little help, or they are operating at too low of a vibration to be able to connect with their loved ones on the other side. And that is what I am here for.

I mentioned it before, but grief, fear, bad habits like smoking, gambling, and watching pornography, and even a bad diet that contains alcohol, fatty and/or processed foods and sugars, can lower your vibration. This makes it very hard for our loved ones to bring forth loving messages to us from the spirit realms.

I am here to help unblock your energy, help you raise your vibration, open your heart and mind, and most importantly, help you increase your faith in God. If you are having a hard time finding peace after losing a loved one, ask God if it would be in your best interest to seek out a medium. If God approves, seek to book an appointment with a lightworker who works for Him. Trust, and have faith that God will guide you in the right direction. I can assure you that the information that comes through in a reading is for your highest good. There has never been anything "bad" that has occurred in any of the readings I have done in my mediumship journey.

Chapter 14
Your Purpose, My Purpose

Every single one of my readings reinforces my belief that we are souls who incarnate here to grow in some way. It seems that we, as souls, learn faster in physical form than we can in our natural state in the spirit world, because of the limitations we have while in a body. This may seem contradictive, but these limitations help us grow and evolve faster because there is not the same kind of resistance while we are in our true form as "spirit."

One thing that seems to be very common among my research of near-death experiences, is that when we pass away, we experience what is called a "life review." It's not by accident that people say, "My life flashed before my eyes," when they have a close brush with death. During this "instant download" of the life review, you will be able to view all the moments of your last life on Earth. You will "relive" all the situations, decisions, and emotions, of every experience — you will "view" a 360-degree perspective of your entire life. As a soul, this is your time to review how you acted throughout your last life, in order to determine if you accomplished the lessons you set out to learn while on Earth.

Many people who make appointments with me for readings, visit with me to simply communicate with their loved ones who have passed away. However, many of those readings turn into some sort of spiritual guidance for the sitter as well. Each reading has led to a variety of spirit messages, but the one central phenomenon is that every sitter seems to receive a significant amount of information that can be extremely helpful to them. Some of the things Spirit has had me express to my clients would blow your mind. I have been told to impart suggestions to sitters that have ranged from starting their own Boys and Girls Club to reconnecting with an ex-boyfriend/girlfriend.

Most of my readings result in the sitter finding, repairing, or strengthening their faith in God. There are also a significant number of readings that guide the sitter toward finding out what their purpose is in this lifetime.

Spirit uses all kinds of people as messengers of God. We are all in this together, and some of us need a little help finding our way through life. As a medium, I am here to help others be the best they can be. This can sometimes mean bringing in the energy of a passed loved one to relay a message, but there are times when I simply pass along important information that the sitter might not otherwise be able to obtain themselves, due to their energy being blocked. This blockage occurs mostly because of the many previously mentioned possible circumstances that may be obstructing the sitter from connecting with Spirit. I have had so many sitters e-mail me after their reading to tell me that the information that came through was exactly what they needed to hear, although, they sometimes admit it wasn't what they expected or even *wanted* to hear.

Each one of us has unique specific things to accomplish while on this journey we call life. Coming to understand my life's purpose at thirty-seven years old was one of the most satisfying experiences of my life. It took a few years and a lot of ups and downs for me to even begin to process this understanding, so be patient with your own discovery.

I encourage you to seek out what your life's purpose is. Whether you are eighteen years old, ninety years old, or somewhere in between, it is never too late to discover what you came here to accomplish and figure out how you can adjust your life to fulfill that mission. Most often, people who are on their highest path, are on it because they are aware of their life's purpose and live in a love-based reality. These souls are the ones who are often asked by God to help others find their path once they find theirs. Making an effort to "remember" your soul's purpose, and working to fulfill that mission, will lead you to experience your best life possible. You will then be better equipped to help others do the same.

How can you discover your life's purpose and start to understand why you are here? Just ask God to show you. "Ask, and it shall be given you; seek, and ye shall find; knock, and it shall be opened unto you." (Matthew 7:7). (NKJV).

Following is a small exercise. If you practice this daily, I firmly believe that you can begin to understand and hear Spirit. This exercise will better enable you to recognize what Spirit is trying to tell you, so you can find your purpose.

Find Your Purpose Exercise:

I highly recommend practicing this daily, for an unspecified amount of time. *Be consistent. Pay attention. Trust.*

Close your eyes and get comfortable. Limit all distractions and focus all your attention on your breathing. Say the following, either aloud or to yourself:

God. . . Please help me discover how I can best serve You. Please enlighten me with the details of my life's purpose. How can I fulfill my mission as a soul while in this body? I am asking with love so I can serve you with conviction and make this world a better place. I am asking for guidance, and I am ready to receive any information that can help me complete my pre-determined goals for this lifetime.

Repeat this exercise daily and pay attention. It will most likely take some time to receive information — and that information may come to you in a variety of ways, such as signs, symbols, or hearing a "voice," etc. Stay consistent, be open-minded, and make your intention completely transparent. Pay attention. You will receive the guidance you need, which may differ from what you seek.

I know I have not said it much, but you do not need a

medium to connect with God/Spirit. Your life is between you and God. I am here, along with other teachers and guides, to help you rekindle or strengthen your relationship with God, so you can live a beautiful life. I think the main reason God uses people like pastors, gurus, teachers, priests, counselors, and even mediums, is because some people get so lost, and they just need some guidance. Messengers of God have been present throughout history to help humanity. And many are here on this Earth right now as you read this.

As I mentioned in Chapter 6, in my opinion, "satan" is nothing more than ego or sin (the opposite of love). I don't believe there is an eternal damnation in "hell." That being said, the illusion of "satan" is "real," and can harm many people. "Satan" comes in the form of drugs, hatred, jealousy, and ego-based thinking, among other things. When you have any thought, action, or decision to make, ask yourself, *Is this love or is this fear?* Fear is the root of all things "satan," and God is all things Love. Don't give in to the negativity in this world. Trust in God and protect yourself. Live in His Love, not in fear. I firmly believe that you don't have to physically die to experience "Heaven." You can experience Heaven right here on Earth.

It takes a lot of love, meditation, forgiveness, patience, and trust, to be on your highest path. I cannot say that I have mastered those things, but I firmly believe that my life is amazing because I make a conscious effort to lead with love at all times. Of course, it is not easy sometimes, but leading with love, in *all situations*, should be a no-brainer at this point, since you have read it just a few times throughout this book. Don't let the temptations of this physical world (i.e., satan), influence your decisions.

Life is so much more than we can understand. So why not lead with love? *Why are you here? How can you make this world a better place? What impact can you have on this world? How can you help others?*

Please continue to ask your spirit guides, God, or whatever you call "Source," what your life's purpose is. *What are you doing here?* You may be surprised by what you see, hear, feel, or begin to know. If you feel like you aren't receiving any answers, keep asking until you do. Answers will come when they are supposed to. Your soul is awakening. The Universe is a vast and awesome system. We may not be fully equipped to understand life as we know it, but I can tell you that asking and finding out why you are here, can be absolutely life changing.

This book is part of *my* life's purpose. At one time, I would never have imagined that I would be an author, teacher, and a medium, but God obviously has a plan for me, and I have fully embraced it.

During the reading I received from Beth, she hinted that being a medium was something I would do to help others in this life. I love helping people, and the healing experienced by Diedre, the woman I had given a reading to in Boston, had left a significant impression on me. Beth had also enabled me to experience how amazing it was to communicate with my deceased father.

Once I understood that mediumship was part of *my* purpose in this life, I recognized that it would be in my best interest to serve God by accomplishing that mission. With direction from Him, I determined it was time to get to work. When you are doing God's work, while at the same time fulfilling your purpose, you will have an extreme excitement and passion while you are doing it. That exhilaration you feel is a sign you are on the right path.

As I started my journey to understand the process and details regarding delivering messages from Spirit, I would absorb book after book about mediumship. I could not put them down. Between May 2017, and June 2018, I focused my attention on understanding how to enhance my abilities as a medium. A lot was going on in my life during this time that I feel you should know. The reason I feel you should know is because there *will always be time to serve God and fulfill your life's purpose.*

It took me well over a year, and a significant amount of time and energy, just to understand how I could best serve God. It took time to fully comprehend the mission He sent me here to accomplish. Be patient. What I want you to understand is that *you are never too busy* to initiate and implement the specifics of *your* purpose, so you accomplish what you came here to do.

Whether you become a medium, go back to school, or

start a non-profit organization, there is always time to do what you feel your soul is urging you to do. Even if you are reading this and you don't think you have much time left on this Earth — or maybe you even know that you don't — this still applies to you. Sometimes, just praying and asking what your purpose is (refer to the exercise earlier in this chapter), can positively affect something or someone in this life or in your next incarnation.

Even though life was extremely busy for me, I still had time to serve God and do what He was asking me to do. What follows, is an explanation of how I started to execute my life's purpose. I hope that by sharing with you how I found my life's purpose, you will be better equipped to find yours.

In March of 2017, my wife gave birth to our third son, Johnny Walker. He was born two weeks after I quit gambling. At the time, I was working as a medical sales rep for a Fortune 500 company. In that same year, I was on a mission to be a President's Club winner, a special distinction that most sales organizations use to recognize elite sales performance. I worked my ass off and ended up achieving President's Club. I was one of the top sales reps in the company that year and I worked very hard to accomplish that.

After a very busy summer with three kids — and with all those health and sleeping issues I mentioned earlier — I went back to my very unfulfilling job. In the fall, another job opportunity came up. To be brief, I was not happy at my existing job at the time, and my work-life balance was not as it should have been. In addition to that, my wife and I had just bought a commercial building that needed a complete rehab. We were also doing some major home renovations on our primary residence and we were traveling a lot as well. To say we were busy would be an understatement.

Still, I continued to read two or three books a week about life, the Universe, reincarnation, souls, God, theology, mediumship, and near-death experiences. In October 2017, I interviewed for a new job and accepted the offered position in late November. I had to go through a month of intense training because this new job was in pharmaceutical sales.

By the spring of 2018, I was well into my new job. At the same time, I was being patient about knowing *for sure* when, or even if, mediumship was something God wanted me to do to help others. The mediumship path felt so right, and I was experiencing some crazy synchronicities during this time. However, I wasn't "getting any messages" or doing any readings. But I still remained patient and trusted I was doing what God wanted me to do.

It wasn't until I signed up for an "understanding mediumship" course in May, that things started to take off. The class was once a week for six weeks. The teacher of the class was a full-time medium who felt he had a calling to teach others about energy work. He taught our class of eight students how to receive and trust subtle messages from Spirit in order to help others.

We started doing readings for each other within the first

two weeks. It was amazing. Even though visiting Beth had made me a believer, there was still some major skepticism on my part about the whole process. This class helped me become more of a believer, and also helped me learn to trust the information I was receiving from Spirit. When it was my turn to give a reading, the messages I passed on were extremely accurate.

I must have impressed the teacher, because he asked me to join him on a Facebook Live event to give free readings to people. Once I started doing Facebook Live readings, my messages continued to get stronger and stronger. When the class ended, I continued educating myself by reading books. I always asked God to lead me to books He wanted me to read. Many of the ways He led me to some of the books were jaw-dropping. I continued to do live readings with my teacher once a week and I noticed that I was getting very accurate, detailed, specific, and helpful information from Spirit.

About a month after the class ended, I had an *urge* to put it out publicly that mediumship was something I was meant to do to help others. I called Beth since she had been a mentor to me throughout my whole learning process. She suggested that before I "came out," I should give some free private readings to get started and see how well they went. I loved the idea of free readings because I had never wanted to charge money anyway. In fact, at first, I thought I would always do free readings because I have a full-time job and I just love helping people. Later in this chapter we will talk more about charging money for readings.

Beth lined up three volunteers and I gave them all free readings. The first one went well and the second one went even better. The third reading was amazing, so I decided to do one more to make sure I felt comfortable charging money for them. That one was incredible too, so after that, I was officially "out!" On June 22, 2018, I announced to everyone via social media, that I was a medium, and my wife built and launched my website.

"Coming out" was one of the hardest things I have ever done. I "came out" because I knew in my heart that mediumship was what God wanted me to do and that it was part of my life's purpose. Don't *ever* let anyone or anything hold you back from fulfilling your purpose and living your dream. When you are in touch with your soul, the things you *want* to do, are the things you came here *to* do. Heart-based thoughts will lead the way, and the ego-based thoughts will slowly start to fade. Always be faithful to God and be who He wants you to be.

I put myself on Facebook and also continued to go live with my teacher. My readings were getting significantly better, which meant I was able to help more people. Pretty soon, people were booking private appointments with me, and my schedule filled up very quickly.

I understood that when I came out as a medium, some people would look at me differently. I knew that some people wouldn't understand what I was doing, and I also accepted that I was putting some of my friendships at risk. Added to that was the fact that in some Christians' eyes, mediumship is pretty much considered the work of the devil. It can be quite difficult at times dealing with critics and skeptics, so now I just send love to all of them because everyone needs it. I simply answer to God and no one else.

If you are reading this book because you are a medium, or you are looking to fulfill your life's purpose, no matter what it is, please take my advice and don't worry about what other people think. Please remember that whatever you do is between you and God. I encourage you to do what is in your heart, because He will speak to you through it.

If you are looking to utilize your God-given gifts as a medium, do not let anyone prevent you from using those gifts to help others. I feel it would be of "satan" to have God-given gifts and to *not* use them to help others. (1 Peter 10-11). No matter what your life's purpose is, please do not let another person's words or actions influence what you know in your heart will help you serve God and at the same time fulfill your dreams. Some people just like bringing others down. Let your light shine (Matthew 5:16), come from a place of love, do your thing, and believe in yourself.

As I write this, I have been a practicing medium for almost two years. As I mentioned earlier, I give away free readings every Monday night on "Monday Night Live with Daniel John," on my Facebook page, "Daniel John Medium." I also volunteer my time, giving many free private readings a few times a month to organizations that help grieving parents who have lost children. I also give three to four private readings per week, along with two to three group readings a month. I have my own studio in town, where I give private and group readings, as well as Reiki treatments. I still have a full-time job as a medical sales rep, but something tells me it won't be very long before God leads me to a new type of career. I do enjoy my current full-time job, so I hope I can continue that for a while longer. However, I feel that everything in this world is all up to God and divine timing.

Ninety-nine percent of my over eight-hundred readings to date, have given the sitter some sort of spiritual guidance that has helped them live a more fulfilling life. There have been a few readings where that did not occur (I don't know what happened), and in those cases, I refunded the sitter's money. My advice to a developing medium would be not to worry about "bad" readings, because they do happen occasionally. If I start a reading, and after twenty minutes, I don't feel like it is flowing, I offer the sitter the opportunity to end the session and tell them I will gladly refund them. If they want to move forward, there will not be a refund on the reading. This has happened maybe twice, and both times the reading went great after that. Before, I would struggle for an hour and try to produce the reading they wanted. Do not do that. It will be a waste of time and energy for both of you, and you will feel extremely tired afterward. Once in a great while, for many unknown reasons, the reading is a dud. That's okay, as long as it is very rare, because "bad" readings should only happen once in a while.

I also recommend becoming a certified medium because the testing for the certification is intense and it can validate your gifts. There are a few well-known certifiers available. I'll never forget when I was going through my certification, I prayed to God for confirmation, because I *always* need it from Him. I would say to Him, *God, if this is the work you want me to do, help me pass this certification. If it is not, I am totally okay with it. So, in that case, guide me to fail, and I will do whatever else you ask of me.* I would pray that same prayer every day throughout the entire month and a half certification process. I passed, and it further confirmed that I am doing His work.

My mediumship certification can be viewed at: https://www.findacertifiedmedium.com/mediums/ny/geneva/daniel-john/

If you are a medium, and you are wondering if you should charge money and how much you should charge, I would suggest starting out by giving a few free readings to friends and/or family. Once you have confidence and recognize that you are delivering accurate messages from Spirit that help others, I highly recommend that you charge sitters for your readings. It's difficult to explain to people who do not do this work, why mediums charge for their services. But I will try.

A significant amount of time and energy goes into a

private reading and they are usually well over an hour long. Since we are energy, and we, as mediums, are working with energy, readings can deplete us of it. Readings can be, and often are, extremely draining. There is also a significant amount of preparation and aftercare involved as well, such as meditation, protection prayers, recording, and then uploading and e-mailing the reading to the sitter. If it is an in-person reading, I must go to my studio, turn on the lights, turn on the heat or air, and set up the room. It takes a lot of time, money, and energy, to provide this service. You will always be asked to do free readings by people who "really need one." Don't let people take advantage of you. Be firm, set your price, and stick to it.

I will say, however, there *have* been multiple times when Spirit has guided me to give a free reading to someone. It has happened twenty or thirty times in about two years, so don't give in to everyone. Just trust that God will nudge you to give a free reading when He would like you to do so.

Occasionally, I will get a message from someone saying that if a medium's ability is a gift from God, I should not be making money from it. We all need to use our time and energy to support ourselves and our families. Football players, engineers, doctors, and people in almost every other profession, are using their God-given gifts to make a living. Some people value what a medium does and will gladly pay you for your time and energy. Some people don't. Stick to your price and don't let others influence you in that respect.

I think this is best explained as a balance thing. The exchange that occurs in any transaction, whether it is for a service or goods, is the way the Universe works. That balanced exchange is important whether it is monetary or not. It is not about the money for me, and I have even exchanged services with other practitioners. Please understand that a medium can't just give free readings all day. It is just not possible or practical. It is a good idea, however, to keep your cost reasonable, even though that is subjective.

If you are using your God-given gifts to help others by performing readings, please know that the messages you receive from Spirit are often extremely subtle. Every medium is different and has their own strengths. Develop and create your *own* unique style. Do not compare yourself to other mediums — just trust in what you receive, pass on the messages, and lead with love. You are doing a great thing.

I cannot tell you how often I receive messages and e-mails telling me how much better a sitter feels after a reading. It is so gratifying to know that God gave me this gift to connect others with their loved ones who are not physically with them anymore. I don't know how it all works and perhaps I never will. I do know, however, that there is an abundant amount of love, compassion, healing, and growth that takes place in every single reading.

It is so exciting to wake up every day and acknowledge that I have another opportunity to serve God and accomplish the mission I came here to complete. You can have this same excitement by finding your purpose as well. Pray and ask. Trust and pay attention to what the Universe is telling you.

Chapter 15
What is a Psychic?

"Can you tell me the future? Can you read my mind?"

Nope and nope. . . And I am glad I can't.

And no. . .I don't know the lottery numbers. . .

People always ask me how it works to be a "psychic." I don't call myself "psychic" because I feel that the word is often misinterpreted. Being "psychic" only means that one can access information by using more than just their five senses. So, technically all mediums have "psychic" abilities, but not all mediums predict the future. Even though all mediums have "psychic" ability, not all "psychics" are mediums (meaning that they can't communicate with the deceased).

According to *Merriam-Webster Dictionary*, "psychic" is defined as "lying outside the sphere of physical science or knowledge: Immaterial, moral, or spiritual in origin or force" or "sensitive to nonphysical or supernatural forces and influences: marked by extraordinary or mysterious sensitivity, perception, or understanding." (Merriam-Webster.com, https://www.merriam-webster.com, 8 May 2011).

Think of "psychic" as the term used to cover all abilities that are not able to be explained with physical science.

Predicting the future, communicating with the deceased, or practicing psychometry, are all forms of "psychic" abilities. Information that is obtained psychically has no reasonable, scientific way to be understood or proven. *Make sense?*

So, my point is, even though I am "psychic," all that means is that I am somehow able to obtain information by using something beyond the normal five senses. (Sometimes referred to as extrasensory perception or ESP). That *does not* mean that I can read your mind, predict the future, or know all things. Every "psychic" has different abilities, but all psychics obtain their information with no logical scientific explanation as to how they obtained it.

As a medium, I have a heightened connection with Source, so I *do* obtain information "psychically." And the information I receive is often extremely helpful to others. I can go days, weeks, or even months (outside of my private readings), without having any real "psychic" experiences. So please know that my spiritual gifts and abilities are that of a medium. I connect with Spirit to pass on messages of love from the "other side," in order to help people here on Earth.

Even though, occasionally, future events *do* sometimes come through in readings, for the sitter's highest good, I do *not* perform psychic (future) readings. I am a servant of God, and I feel that my responsibility is to use my gifts from Him to help the people that He puts in front of me. I still receive e-mails from people who ask about their future love life or work life, and I tell them to seek God, not a psychic or medium, for that kind of guidance. In my readings, I simply pass along whatever messages Spirit wants me to communicate, because the sitter is severely grieving, and/or unable to connect with Source themselves at that point in their life.

Remember, my goal as a medium is to rekindle my sitter's trust and faith in God, help heal their grief, spread God's Love, and to help them understand that eternal life exists. I don't allow my sitters to ever book another paid, private reading with me again, and at the same time, I highly recommend that they wait six months before booking with another medium. I am a big supporter of working with God to navigate through your life. I am simply put here to guide you to that path with Him.

Even though I "communicate with the dead," I lead a pretty normal life. Most of the time, I am just like everyone else, and don't experience anything out of the ordinary in my everyday life. I enjoy playing with my kids, spending time with my wife, reading books, and listening to music. I do not communicate with Spirit on a regular basis, even though messages occasionally do come through in public. Even in my readings, messages come in so subtly, it is quite difficult to tell if messages are from Spirit or from my own thoughts. That is why I seriously want as little information as possible about my sitters, before, and even during a reading.

Even though most people aren't able to communicate with Spirit regularly, I believe that every single one of us has the natural ability to do so. Have you ever thought about someone, and then five seconds later they call you? Have you ever found yourself singing a song and then it is the next song that plays on the radio? Have you ever gone to answer your phone before it rings? These are all examples of intuition. Intuition is a natural ability to just "know" things. Some people have higher degrees of intuition based on several contributing factors, but no one is without it. I use my intuition to serve God, so I can live my life on my highest path and help others do the same.

There are many books available on how you can increase your intuition, but I will say that eating right, exercising, meditating, having faith in God, having compassion for others, practicing forgiveness, and leading with love, will help strengthen it. In addition to helping others, I use my intuition in many areas of my life, including work, relationships, and even staying safe while driving. Intuition is one of God's many gifts to you, so it would be in your best interest to use it. Always remember to use your intuition, while coming from a place of love, with nothing but good intentions toward everyone with whom you interact.

Chapter 16
I See Dead People

How does it all work? And what is a medium, anyway? The word *medium* means "halfway between two extremes." What mediums do is connect the two extremes of this world and the spirit world. As I have mentioned, mediumship and life after death were not things I believed in before all this happened to me. I figured that we live, then we die, and then we go to Heaven or hell. Either way, I didn't think that we could, or should, communicate with people who had passed away. Well, I was "dead" wrong. And if you are wondering, I don't actually *see* dead people. . .and I'm glad I don't.

I am the first to admit that communicating with someone who has died is hard to believe, and just kind of weird. It is not easy to describe, and it is sometimes quite difficult to prove to skeptics. It took many books and readings for me to begin to understand what mediumship is and how it all works. As a skeptic, I watched shows like *Long Island Medium* and *Crossing Over* to see if they were staged, if people were somehow lying, or if it was all a trick. It wasn't until I went to a medium myself that I became a true believer. I not only came to believe in the reality of mediumship, but I also started to recognize that readings can be extremely beneficial to people who need love and guidance in their life.

Earlier, I touched on what happened at my first-ever appointment with a medium, but I think a little more detail of that reading will benefit you.

Beth is a local, well-respected woman, who has been a practicing medium for over twenty years, so I chose her — or maybe Spirit did — for my first reading. Even though I had already given a reading "out of nowhere" to my co-worker, Deidre, in Boston, I went in as a skeptic, but I came out a believer. Beth mentioned things she absolutely could not have known without getting an authentic message from my loved ones in spirit. I tested her, limited my responses, watched her facial expressions, listened to her tone, and observed her posture. She was accurate, sincere, honest, and direct. As hard as it was to believe, I was ultimately convinced without a doubt, that she was actually communicating with some of my family in spirit.

The twenty or thirty validations she gave me that day were very specific and extremely detailed. Through Beth, my dad shared amazingly healing messages. She asked me what was up with the garage door? That was a private joke between my dad and me. She asked me who was the bowler, Ralph? That was my great Uncle Ralph, who not only bowled a 300 game, but he used to take me bowling. She validated things related to my life and career as well. Some things she relayed to me, were not validated until after the reading, and one specific significant thing took almost six months to be validated. When that validation occurred, it was so amazing I can't even explain it.

Here, I will try to explain how mediumship works, at least for me anyway: I do not have verbal conversations with spirits and I very rarely hear them audibly. I do not see them, and the communications are extremely subtle. When I first started practicing mediumship, I found that the messages were so subtle they were hard to trust. Most of the time, Spirit does not use actual words. They usually use pictures, symbols, and feelings to impress my thoughts, so I can relay information to the sitter. I try to determine what the spirit is trying to convey to their loved ones. I often compare spirit communication to a game of charades. I also find that the person who passed away, is just as excited to communicate with the sitter as the sitter is to communicate with the deceased.

You will find that most mediums have what we call a "spirit dictionary." These are symbols Spirit uses to help relay the information for dissemination. I will give you a few examples so you can grasp the idea.

When Spirit "shows me" in my mind's eye, a raisin, that is their way to make me mention California, or my signal that I have to talk about actual raisins. When they show me a cane, it means the spirit wants to tell the sitter that they do not want them to remember how the deceased looked right before they passed, but to instead focus on the healthy times. When they show me a brick, the loved one in spirit wants to confirm that they passed quickly (like a falling brick), although it occasionally means that I need to mention actual bricks (like the house the deceased lived in).

When they show me a bell, the spirit wants to thank the sitter for taking care of them when they were sick, although one in every ten times, it means I have to talk about an actual bell. When they show me the number "73," it is usually a father energy coming through because that is how old my dad was when he passed. It can also mean that I have to mention "73," which could be an age, a year, or even July 3rd (7/3).

When they show me Twinkies®, I must talk about twins or actual Twinkies®. I just did a reading yesterday when this came up. Not only were Twinkies® the spirit's favorite food, he had a twin brother with him on the "other side," and that twin wanted to come through as well. Spirit can get very "punny!"

Once I obtain the symbol, I usually get a "feeling" along with it. I will pass on what I see, feel, or sense, along with an interpretation of what I think it may mean. Then, the sitter will let me know if the information makes sense to them and how they understand it. It is so cool, because for instance, when I "see" a raisin, they often will confirm that their loved one was born in California, and at the same time, they just booked a trip yesterday to go visit the Golden State. Then, as the reading progresses, the information continues to flow, and it can get very specific and detailed, especially if the sitter is energetically open and full of love. It is neat, for lack of a better word, to experience firsthand communication between the "living" and the "dead."

Over the last year and a half, I have experienced some things I cannot even begin to explain. The amount of absolute pure love and healing within each reading is beyond words.

Spirit uses all kinds of ways to communicate whatever is for the highest good of the sitter. They have communicated songs, numbers, times, objects, specific detailed experiences, full names, names of streets, nicknames, and even private jokes or sayings.

I'll never forget the time when I was doing a reading for a woman and I told her I was getting the name, "Bob" or "Robert." She insisted she knew no one with the name. I told her that it was strong, and she continued to say, "No." I moved on, which I rarely do because sometimes it just takes some thinking for the sitter to validate what is coming through. Then, I told her I was getting the name, "Eleanor" or "Ellie." She then told me that her friend, Ellie, who she wanted to connect with, had passed away a few months prior. What she said next really made me laugh.

"That's funny, Daniel, because her name was Ellie Bob!"

That was the only time I can remember that I received a full name, but Spirit has been getting better at giving me full first names as I have continued to grow and trust. There is nothing like sitting down and getting the name of a passed loved one right off the bat, although that is not always the case. Sometimes, the spirit will give me middle names when their first name is a common name like "John," "Mary," or "Mike." In some cases, if the name is obscure and there is no way I can interpret the name, they will show me pictures, sounds, or even groups of letters. They will often give me names of living loved ones as well, because they want to "talk" about them right away.

Sometimes spirit must get very creative to get messages to their loved ones. One time I "saw" Howie Mandell in my mind. As it turned out, the sitter's brother, who had passed away a few months prior, was named "Howdy," so "Howie" is how he chose to come through. One time I had a spirit show me a picture of the painting, "American Gothic," only to find out that the sitter actually has a picture of her parents mimicking this classic painting, on the wall in her living room. This was their way to come through. Spirit is more creative than I can even explain.

It is so amazing, because the information that Spirit passes on to us is so full of love and compassion. Spirit often illustrates that they are very present in their loved one's current life. Because I only communicate with energies that are at a high vibration, or in "Heaven," all messages are of love and for the sitter's highest good. Occasionally, however, I do have to pass on information that is uncomfortable to say. However, in all cases, it is *always* for the sitter's highest good, even though it can sometimes be quite difficult for them to hear.

I remember one occasion where a spirit communicated with me that he chose to die in a car accident earlier, rather than later in his death window, because it would be significantly easier for his family. I have also had spirit tell me things like the sitter is not parenting the best way they can, or that they have not completely grieved their loved one's loss. One time, a loved one in spirit, wanted to tell the sitter that they were going down the wrong path in life and it was time to make a change. No matter what comes through, it's *always* for the sitter's benefit.

Occasionally, spirit chooses the most obscure way of communicating what they want the sitter to know. Here is an example: I was giving a reading to a woman who had lost her dad. Her father came through right away and had me say, "Jeffery or Justin." The woman said her ex-husband was "Jeffery," and that her current husband was "Jody." I said, "I feel that Dad wants to talk about the ex." I passed on some detailed messages to her, about the timing of her divorce and her dad's passing, which she validated. What happened next was something I still talk about to this day.

In my mind, I "heard" the song, "Summer of '69," by Bryan Adams. Now, I had not heard that song in a long time, so I knew it must be coming from Spirit. I asked her if the song meant anything to her and she responded with, "No." I asked her if Bryan Adams, or the year 1969, or the number "69," meant anything to her and she still could not relate. Then, in my mind, I asked Spirit if I could move on, and they gave me a hard, "No." *Okay*, I thought.

"We can't leave this song," I told her. She still had no idea what it meant. As I started to sing the lyrics in my head, I realized that in the song, the lyrics are "Jimmy quit, Jody got married." I said to her, "Oh my gosh. . .did your dad miss the wedding with your current husband, Jody?"

She replied with, "Yes he did."

I said, "He is saying, 'No, he didn't. This is his way to tell you he was at the wedding in spirit."

How crazy is that? Then, as if it couldn't get any cooler, I told her that I was seeing a star or stars. She did not understand this. For about a minute, we could not figure it out, and then she had an epiphany.

"Oh, my God," she said. "I took my dad's jacket and cut out a star design from it and placed it on my wedding dress, so I could have him with me."

"Wow!" I said.

This was her dad's way to show her that he was with her in spirit and he did not miss her wedding.

I will never forget the time when a spirit had me mention the song, "Stayin Alive," by the Bee Gees. I mentioned the song to my sitter, and she proceeded to tell me that exact song was the song her mother had requested her family to play at her funeral. That was her mother saying, "Thank you for fulfilling my wishes!"

I could give you so many examples that would give you goosebumps, but it would be better to watch some actual readings on my YouTube channel or Facebook page.

I have had some readings that are very heavy and quite hard to accomplish. Many of my readings are for parents who have lost a child. I've also had a few readings where the sitter has lost multiple children. Those readings can be extremely difficult. I do get emotional on occasion. However, I must put my emotions aside and pass on messages that often have life-changing results. I am honored to have this gift, and I feel blessed to be one of the mediums through which Spirit chooses to help bring messages of comfort to the grieving.

People often don't realize what a major responsibility it is to do this work. "But he who did not know, yet committed things deserving of stripes, shall be beaten with few. For everyone to whom much is given from Him, much will be required; and to whom much has been committed, of him they will ask more." (Luke 12:48). (NKJV).

I am a man of God with high ideals and respect for Him. I understand that everything I say, do, and feel, is part of something way bigger than me. I trust in God and my spirit guides to guide me with my readings and in my life. I fully understand I am doing His work and that this "job" is something He is asking me to do.

I must protect myself with His Love and Light and trust that He is keeping me safe. I have been doing readings for almost two years and have *never* encountered a negative/evil spirit. I can't claim that I "know for certain" that I haven't, but my statement is based upon my many readings and experiences. I can't stress enough how every single reading is so full of love,100% of the time.

Mediumship is often energy-draining for everyone involved, so as I previously mentioned, it is vitally important to not only protect myself, but my sitters as well. I must make sure that I balance my personal life and work-life, so I can serve God with every ounce of energy I have. I feel that God and my spirit guides provide the support I need to do His work. Even though mediumship can be difficult and draining at times, it is so rewarding to use my God-given gift to help others in such a profound way.

Chapter 17
Diet...Diet?

I am including a chapter on diet in this book because what we eat has a major effect on our bodies. Studies have proven that an unhealthy diet, in combination with a lack of exercise, can lead to obesity, disease, and even death. What you may not realize is that because we are made of energy, what we ingest has a significant energetic effect on us.

I cannot stress how beneficial it is to eat right and exercise regularly. When you take care of your body and your energy properly, you will operate at a higher vibration, and therefore, allow yourself to be more open to helpful messages from Spirit.

After college, I received my certification as a personal trainer. I chose to concentrate on nutrition because I found it very interesting. I am no longer a certified personal trainer, nor am I a nutritionist or a doctor, but I would like to share some basic knowledge with you about your diet, so you can increase your energetic vibration.

My suggestions are not a replacement for asking your doctor for a personal, customized, program to fit your individual needs. However, what follows, is a basic guide to healthy eating, so you can move toward your best quality of life, limiting disease, and tuning into your higher self.

I want to start by sharing with you what foods are best to avoid. It may be common sense to you, but in case it isn't, I will list them.

Always Avoid or Extremely Limit:

- Fast food
- Deep-fried food
- Processed food
- Foods that contain preservatives
- Non-natural sugars
- High-fat foods
- Soda
- Alcohol
- Sweet drinks
- High-calorie foods like creams, candy, cookies, and ice cream

I know, I know, I've just nixed all the good stuff, right? I'm not saying you can't ever have these things but limiting them will help you tremendously. Eating healthy is not easy, and it can sometimes mean spending more money, but the return on investment is well worth it, especially in the long run.

Following, I have listed some foods that are very good for you. I highly encourage you to add more of them to your diet.

Foods to Enjoy:

- Fruits
- Vegetables
- Beans
- Nuts
- Lean meats (like chicken or fish)
- Eggs
- Grains
- Unprocessed foods

If you don't know how to tell if a food is processed, check the list of ingredients. If you can identify all the ingredients on the list, you're on the right track. If you don't know many of them, or can't pronounce them, it might be a good idea to stay away, because they are usually chemical designations, and you are looking at processed food.

There is no perfect diet to follow, but the best way to know your own optimal and personalized diet is to check with a doctor or hire a nutritionist. Your diet is just one piece of the puzzle to being on your highest path. Staying healthy helps you vibrate at the highest frequency possible (pure love). Many people struggle with diet, but please know there are many healthy foods available that taste great. I hope this information helps you make conscious, well-researched choices in order to better enable you to strike a balance in what you eat.

When it comes to drinking, anything other than water is usually not the best choice. There is always room for tea, coffee, or a glass of wine, but sodas and juices are not ideal. Some juices, like orange and grapefruit, are high in vitamins and minerals, but in my opinion, they should be used in moderation. Treat yourself occasionally to a fruit drink or even a cold beer, but it would be to your benefit to make it an occasional choice. Water is always the best option, and it would be in your best interest to drink it 95% of the time. When you consume any drink that has calories, they are empty calories because they add to your daily caloric intake without providing much, if any, nutritional value. I also recommend that you stay away from diet sodas.

And yes, alcohol is not only taxing on your liver and other organs, it also lowers your vibration significantly. I do not drink much anymore, because I like to be present and have conscious control over what I am doing and thinking, so I can make rational, logical, God/Love based decisions.

Enjoy the fruits of the Earth, and just remember, it is all about moderation and balance.

A Few More Basic Rules:

- Eat smaller portions
- Eat slowly
- Chew more
- Savor each bite
- Don't eat late at night
- Take a probiotic
- Monitor your calories
- Fast intermittently, if your doctor supports it, and your research leads you to believe it could be beneficial for you
- Drink plenty of water
- Plan your meals and snacks to avoid unhealthy eating

I can't stress enough, that eating properly, and exercising, will benefit your physical health, mental health, and your overall energy. The foods I've listed as ones to avoid can not only drain your energy, they can cause undesired inflammation in your body. They can negatively affect your chakras, your attitude, and they can also make you feel sluggish or even cause disease. As a medium, and as someone who recognizes that we are energy, I feel that we operate at our best when we eat a healthy diet. I am not perfect when it comes to diet, or anything else for that matter, but I succeed at eating healthy overall. These dietary suggestions will help you in the short and long term. A healthy dietary lifestyle will also allow you to prove to yourself that you have the willpower and determination needed to make the right choices and not succumb to temptations. This can, and will, carry over into making other good and positive choices in life. Please check with your physician before implementing anything mentioned in this chapter.

Chapter 18
This One's for You, Dad

I would like to give my father his own chapter in this book because I feel that he can help you understand a few very important things about life. My dad is a big reason why I am who I am today. He influenced me significantly before he passed away and continues to have a significant impact on my life, just as much, if not more, in the years since he transitioned.

My father was born in 1941. He was an only child, and when he was nine years old his father abandoned him and my grandmother. My grandma had to work three jobs just to keep a roof over their heads. So, my dad was raised by his grandparents who were from Italy and did not speak English. My dad used to tell me many stories about his early life and how it felt to be raised without a father. I honestly think that one of his goals in life was to give me the love a father *should* give his child since he did not receive it from his father. Showing me love was what my dad did best.

My dad was loving and fun, and he always cared about me. That being said, he was impatient, immature, and financially irresponsible. On his deathbed, he told me that he did not want me to end up like him. He said he wanted more for me and expressed his disappointment in the realization that he hadn't done much with his own life. He did a lot for me and I appreciate that. He taught me that I wanted to be the things that he wasn't, and at the same time, he helped me realize that I also wanted to give my children the same love and silly humor he gave to me.

My dad and I had an "interesting" relationship. He was more like a friend than a father to me. A few years after he and my mom divorced, he told me he was gay and that he had a boyfriend. I remember being embarrassed about it and wanting to change him. At that time, I was sure that God did not approve of homosexuality and, in turn, I believed Dad would go to hell for eternity. *Oh, how a little research, open-mindedness, and time can change one's perspective.*

My dad would bring me around all his friends who were often drinking and doing drugs. I think his intention was simply to help me feel like I was being included in his life. It was probably not a good idea for him to bring a twelve-year-old to a house where people came to purchase and do drugs. However, it did teach me many lessons. Regardless of the details of his more questionable choices, his love, and his effort to be present in my life, were both very transparent. I valued the fact that he wanted to have me around.

In my teens, I would resent the fact that Dad was not helping me financially as other fathers did. We would often get into arguments about it, and he would always say that other fathers could pay for things, but he could give me something better: Love. He was right. Throughout high school and college, we called each other almost every day. My dad was very present at my baseball games, bowling matches, and graduations. He even visited me in college many times.

As I grew older, I started to accept that Dad was going to be the way he was, and at least he loved me. I paid for most, if not all, of the activities we did together, whether it was a meal or one of the ten Steve Miller Band concerts we attended. When I graduated college and was busy with life and friends, we always made time for each other.

Dad did not take care of himself. He ate what he wanted and was a type 2 diabetic. He loved his "fry cakes," and had zero discipline when it came to diet. He endured several amputations, beginning with the toes on his right foot, and continued when doctors removed his left leg from the knee down. He also endured several heart attacks, but somehow, he kept surviving and had a positive attitude most of the time.

In his early seventies, Dad started to get sick. That was when I had to step in and give him the love and support he always gave me. He lived in my grandma's house after she passed away, and it was getting to be too much for him to take care of. In March 2014, he was admitted to the hospital with an infection, and his health began to rapidly decline.

My dad made me power of attorney and selected me as the sole executor of his will and estate (which had a negative balance). My sister decided to take herself out of the equation since she had not been speaking to our family for quite some time. It was all me and Dad, and we were in it together. He needed a lot of attention and it was a very stressful time. I learned many things while figuring out how to take care of someone who had no money or insurance and was unable to live alone.

As we started to figure out his finances and housing, things took a turn for the worse. In June 2014, after months of e-mailing and visiting lawyers, financial support organizations, and housing assistance companies, Dad was diagnosed with stage 4 pancreatic cancer. He was given three to six months to live. Instead of moving into the apartment I had *finally* secured for him, he had to remain in the hospital for treatments. He tried to fight for a week or so, but he soon admitted to me that he was "ready to go." I will never forget the moment when he told me was giving up the fight!

I visited Dad almost daily, and we got to spend some quality time together, even though I had to witness the cancer slowly take over his body. He lost weight, his color changed, and he was not eating much. As hard as it was to watch him decline, I felt so blessed to be able to say goodbye to him. In early September that same year, he was moved into hospice.

On October 1, I went to visit Dad for what would be the last time. I held his hand and told him I loved him. Somehow, I knew I would never see him again. I stayed for about an hour before leaving to go pick up my son. As I pulled into my driveway, the hospice nurse called to inform me that my dad passed away about thirty minutes after I'd left. He was gone.

Or so I thought.

As you would expect, it took some time to grieve for Dad and realize he was never going to physically be here again. I would pick up the phone to call him, forgetting that he was gone. I missed being able to talk to him. I'd had him my whole life, and I felt an emptiness deep inside that was hard to accept. I would cry often, which I now know is an essential part of the grieving process.

I mentioned before that the messages that came through from my dad during my session with Beth, were what turned me from a skeptic to a believer. She brought up things only Dad and I knew. She mentioned private jokes and specific information that you can't find on the Internet. I left that reading with so much peace and love in my heart, because I knew for certain that my dad was somehow still with me. I didn't know how, and I didn't know where he was, but he was able to pass messages to me through a medium.

The love that transpired between my father and me in that original reading with Beth, is one of the reasons I do what I do today. My dad connected with me that day in a way I will never forget.

After I started to educate myself about the afterlife, Dad was able to make his presence more known without me having to go to a medium. Because I was meditating, I was operating at a higher vibration, which enabled him to communicate with me more easily. He visited me in more dreams, and we started to have a dialogue. When I say "dialogue," please don't confuse that with spoken words, because it is nothing like that. These communications are very subtle, telepathic kinds of thoughts. I know they are from him because of the many validating experiences I have had.

I want to share one of the many examples of how Dad has communicated with me: While in meditation on an airplane, when I was traveling for work, I felt Dad's presence. Because this occurs through thoughts, and nothing more, it can, and most often feels like you are just making things up in your head. In thought, he said to me, "Buckle your seatbelt." I intuitively felt he meant that my mediumship was going to be a growing responsibility and that it would bring me to places I had never imagined. For some unknown reason, I became extremely emotional. As I questioned the validity of this whole experience, he replied with a thought of, "Open your eyes."

Now, at this point, I definitely thought I was making all this up. *What was I going to do, open my eyes and see his little face floating or something?* I was sure I'd fabricated this whole "conversation" in my head but humored myself by opening my eyes anyway. What do you think was the first thing I saw? *No, not his little head floating.* I opened my eyes and immediately saw the "fasten your seatbelt" sign on the tray table.

A skeptic may chalk that up to coincidence, or even think that maybe it was a subliminal suggestion, because I had seen that sign before I closed my eyes. However, after all the experiences I have had, and because I am operating at a high vibration, I know better.

My dad makes his presence known to me almost every day. This may sound crazy, but he often visits me as a fruit fly, and has told me he can actually manifest them. Animals and insects are a way through which Spirit, or spirits, can choose to communicate with us. Please know that when any animal "visits" you, and you think of a loved one, they are not the actual animal. Our loved ones can influence our thoughts, and since energy is all connected, they can influence animals' thoughts as well. You will be nudged, by receiving a thought from your loved one, to look at an animal and think of them. This is very common, and it would be to your benefit to pay attention to everything around you, including plants.

Spirits often choose to communicate with us through animals, such as cardinals and other birds, butterflies, dragonflies, other insects, ladybugs, or even deer. Our loved ones can also leave us coins or feathers, and they can even mess with electronics. As I mentioned, for some reason, Dad often visits me by showing me a fruit fly. I see them everywhere at very specific, meaningful times in my life. He also plays me Steve Miller Band songs at the craziest times. I got a vasectomy after our third child was born and the exact second the doctor came into the room, the song, "The Joker," played on the radio. I knew Dad was with me.

Be open, pay attention, and trust what you receive. Our

loved ones are often trying to reach out to us to send love and support while we navigate our path here on Earth.

My dad has visited me directly, but he has also come to me through four different mediums as well. Being on the receiving end of such in-depth readings is amazing to me, even being a medium myself. Dad has given me so much validation and love from the other side that it is hard to explain. He has guided and supported me in what I am doing as a medium. He has guided me in my career as well, and often reminds me of certain things that help me live life on my highest path.

I would like to gently remind you that even though it is good to connect with someone who has passed away by consulting a medium, you do not *have* to do so. If you lead with love, pray to God, are kind to others, do not hold grudges, are compassionate, and live life at a high vibration, you can and will receive love and guidance from Spirit all on your own. I know I have repeated that multiple times, but I want it to sink in. I lean on Spirit every single day, so I can live the best life I can live. You have the ability to do the same thing by absorbing and practicing what I have discussed in this book.

A Final Word

I hope that this book leaves you with more answers than questions. There are things in life that sometimes don't make sense to us. When we incarnate on Earth, we have amnesia in a sense. We don't remember who we really are or what we need to do to accomplish our mission while we are here. We can rediscover who we are by trusting and having faith in a Higher Source. The Universe has your back, and it will guide you if you are open to it. Lead with love and ask God for guidance. Remember that there are only two choices in this world: Love or fear. Choose love and live your dream life.

We do not die. Our loved ones are with us even though we cannot see them. We often miss our loved ones, but we must trust that they are not too far away. In fact, they are right here with us! God has a plan, and we are all part of it. Every single one of us can live a life we thoroughly enjoy. Please know that abundance is truly available to all.

Be kind to others, and always come from a place of love. Remember that we are all One and we come from the same Source. In my opinion, there is no better thing to do in this world than to be loving toward others. We all know the fear-based things, right? We shouldn't kill, steal, lie, cheat, judge, envy, or be rude to others. We do know that we should smile, love, forgive, share, care, help, have compassion for others, listen, be kind, be patient, and just be good human beings. It's not always easy to do but making a conscious effort to do the right thing goes a very long way. If you meditate, get enough rest, eat properly, treat others how you want to be treated, take care of yourself, and you are thankful for your blessings, you will live your absolute best life. It's not about what happens *to* you — that is the "victim consciousness." It is about how you choose to look at what happens. *That* is "love consciousness."

I want to end this book by urging you to continue to have an open mind. Explore the possibilities. There is a good chance that even though you don't visually see or understand something, it could still exist. There is a significant amount of value in getting uncomfortable and looking outside the box. That is one of the reasons I can be on my highest path, and why, in turn, I can help others do the same. I could have been set in my ways, limited by other people's opinions, and not open to new knowledge. If I hadn't been paying attention or didn't have the relationship that I do with God, I would not be able to be where I am today.

We all have our own beliefs, and it is our right to have them. Remember to be respectful of others and *their* beliefs, even if they are different than yours.

I am honored and blessed that God has given me this gift and I enjoy every second I get to spend here on Earth, sharing it with people like you. Thank you so much for being part of my journey. *Spread Love. Choose Love. Be Love!*

Testimonials

I would like to share seven testimonials from some of the sitters who have had readings with me. My main purpose in adding these stories is to illustrate the significant healing that transpires in a reading, help you comprehend the power of God/Spirit, and help you understand *how* our loved ones communicate with us from "the other side."

These stories were written by seven different sitters, who did their best to put into words, how impactful their readings were on their lives. They explain how their reading enhanced their ability to live their best life, and/or increased their faith in God.

These testimonials are just a small sample of what I experience daily. Mediumship readings are so full of love, healing, forgiveness, and compassion. I firmly believe that a mediumship reading can provide just as much, if not more, than years of traditional therapy.

Each story is unique, but they all have one common theme. You guessed it. . .love. Take your time and read through them with an open heart and open mind.

The first testimonial is from Marcie. She is one of the most beautiful souls I have encountered on this Earth. Her son, Gregor, passed away at just four years old:

I received the most awesome reading from Daniel

John. I have been to many mediums, but none were as detailed and spot-on as Daniel. He validated everything from events to names, and he also named my brother, Howdy, who shared his appreciation of my protective ways for him when he was passing.

*The things Daniel John said made me realize that he was actually communicating with my son, Gregor, who passed at just four years old. Gregor talked about his time in the sandbox, his love for **Cheez-Its®**, and how I found them months later. He talked about falling with a parachute, and Daniel did not know anything about my son. Gregor actually fell to his death many years prior, and the parachute helped me know that he was at peace about his passing and the details behind it.*

My worry that my son would be upset with me for leaving his father after he passed away was abolished when Daniel helped me understand that Gregor knew and supported my decision.

Daniel threw me for a loop when he said, "Who is Bruce?" out of the blue. That is my current husband's name, and there is no way he would know that! And although I didn't meet Bruce until after Gregor passed, my son had Daniel tell me that he wanted to thank Bruce for "being the husband that my dad couldn't." He sure does treat me like a queen, and I could not deny that my son was knowledgeable about my new husband and was happy about the relationship.

My son's message that came through Daniel about

Gregor being his sister's angel (which I always knew but was now validated), was spot-on! I cannot express in words the peace and feeling of relief I received from the reading, not only for me, but for my daughter as well. She was only two years old when Gregor passed away and she always wondered about her brother. She found it very comforting to know that her brother is her guardian angel.

Thank you, Daniel, for changing my life and giving me peace, validation, and confirmation that my son is happy where he is. God Bless you!

You can view this reading on my YouTube channel: https://youtu.be/SkYek6JIUHY

The second testimonial is from Samantha. It is funny how I forget certain readings and all the details of them, but then there are readings I remember like it was yesterday. This was one I remember very vividly. Please read what Samantha has to say about her reading with me:

Daniel's reading was mind-blowing to say the least. I always believed, or I should say, I wanted to believe, but there was always that shimmer of doubt. . .could this be real? I was going through one of the hardest times of my life. I was a newly single mom to four kids. We lost, Tracey, the father of my two oldest children, to cancer in May 2018.

My kids were 9,5,19 months, and 4 months old, when I had the reading done. Things were hard. I had been watching Daniel online since he started his show. There was always

something that drew me to come back to him every Monday night on his Facebook page. As soon as Daniel started talking about the validation points, I knew it was for me. How could these many things line up? How could he know what he knew? I was hesitant to speak up, but I did. And Spirit led Daniel to talk to me. And that's where it all started.

Some validations Daniel brought forth: The horse on a stick – my daughter's favorite toy. "Pin the Tail on the Donkey" – we had played that game with her dad at her last birthday. Four leaf clovers – Tracey and I used to take Zach looking for them always. On a walk, at a bus stop, we were always telling him to look for them as they would bring him good luck. Number "13" was the year my daughter was born (2013), and then, as I'm writing this, I also realize that Tracey and I were together for 13 years.

Again, how could all this resonate so much? How could he know all this that meant so much to me? Within the first two minutes the tears were flowing from my eyes. I knew that somehow Tracey was with Daniel. I knew he was trying to tell me something. The minute Daniel brought up my hatred for dusting. . .well, I knew without a doubt it was Tracey. I mean, who likes dusting? But I HATED it, and Tracey used to get so annoyed with me. Of course, he would bring this up. He was always one to make me laugh behind my tears. The tears turned into a laugh, with me saying, "Of course he would say that." I still don't like dusting!

Daniel said, "You don't smile anymore." No, I didn't. I

was hurting so bad. My children were 9 and 5 and we had lost their dad 6 months ago. I also had a 1.5-year-old and a 4-month-old baby. Smiling didn't come easy. Pain filled my days. This was the reminder I needed to smile again. I referenced a picture I had posted a few days before, and the caption was "Trying to learn to smile again." There is no way that Daniel could know this, but Tracey did! He was watching us. He was still trying to be a helpful hand from the other side. As Daniel said – Tracey was helping to raise our kids from the other side.

  It got real at this point. It got deep. Daniel told me Tracey said I don't have to be sorry anymore. At this point I can tell you that there was not a single ounce of doubt left in my mind. This was a message that no one in the world could know I needed. No one could know why I needed that message. We had many ups and downs. I was far from perfect. He was far from perfect. But to know he was releasing me of the guilt I had, well. . .watch the reading, you will see how deeply it hit me. I felt like he was sitting right in front of me. I could hear his voice. Tracey told Daniel to tell me to "get back to me." If only Daniel knew how much that was true. I did nothing for me. It all goes back to the smile. I was just a robot getting through the days, but hearing his message made me push to find "me" again. . .to shine, to smile again.

  Then, Daniel referenced a "C" name. The only one was Caiden, my son. Daniel then asked if my oldest, Zach, takes care of him a lot. Oh, yes, he does! They are closer than ever, and with eight years apart in age, their bond is amazing. Zach makes sure he tells his brother all about his dad every day.

Tracey and I had split three years before he passed. We had not been on good terms until he got sick. At which point we put all our differences aside and became a team and became friends again. When Daniel brought up running, running from things. . .it described our relationship to a "T." We both ran. We both never wanted to take blame. See, this is where, "You don't have to be sorry," comes in all over again. This was validation that no one else could have given. There's no way a stranger would know all this.

There's one line that will always stick with me. "Zach will be your rock." Well. . . he is. He is my everything. "He's gotta be the little man of the family," Daniel said. Those were Tracey's EXACT words to Zach.

Then, Daniel referenced a song. It was, "Here We Go Again" by White Snake. Anyone who knew Tracey would know this song, but to me it was the message behind the song that had meaning. "Here we go again on this road, a road I've learned to walk alone." This, for me, was a message all in itself. It's a song that plays over and over in my head now when the days are hard. It reminds me that Tracey is still here with us.

Just when I thought the reading was over, Daniel referenced waking up at 2 AM. I was getting up at 2 AM every single day, but not because my kids were up. I would just get woken up and look at the time and roll back over. Daniel relayed Tracey's comment: "It's me and I'm still going to call you, "Baby." Yup, that's my Tracey. "There's that smile," Tracey relayed through Daniel. Yes, Tracey, you can still make me smile from the other side.

What's amazing is, a few days after the reading, I stopped being woken up at 2 AM. I almost felt like Tracey knew I got the message and he didn't need to try to get my attention anymore. (As a single mom with babies, I appreciated the sleep back).

Not only did Daniel give me an amazing reading that gave me chills and brought healing tears, it also brought so much reassurance. Daniel gave me hope when I was losing all hope.

The next morning, I was in Walmart with my best friend. I was just putting my hand on the box of Lucky Charms® thinking of Daniel telling me that Tracey wants my daughter to "start eating Lucky Charms® again, because "it was their thing." As soon as I went to put the cereal in my cart, my phone beeped, and it was Daniel messaging me to validate a few more things from Tracey. I could not believe that he messaged me in that exact moment. My best friend and I were in shock. It was meant to be. We couldn't believe how much validation came from this one reading with Daniel.

Fast forward a few months after the reading, to when I took my oldest son to his therapy appointment. We were working on a memory book we had started previously about Tracey. When I opened the book, I saw clear as day written,

"Always remember you got this." If you listen to my reading, this was something Daniel brought up word for word! Tracey reminded me, through Daniel, that he always told me this, and the proof was right there in my son's book.

Our journey continued. One day I messaged Daniel just because something crossed my mind, so I felt I had to reach out. He asked me if the song, "Mmmm Bop," meant anything to me. I couldn't believe it! I had just showed my kids that song and told them it was a boy band that Mommy used to drive Daddy crazy with, just to bug him. Daniel kept getting that song in another reading and couldn't make sense of it, until I messaged, and then it all made so much sense.

Spirit is real. Daniel took every ounce of doubt away. Spirit is there when you need them most, and Daniel's gift to bring them closer to you is one that is truly inspiring. To say he changed my life is an understatement.

Samantha, and the reading for her and her family, hold a special place in my heart. It was one of my favorite and most powerfully healing readings I have done to this day.

You can watch Samantha's reading on my YouTube channel: https://youtu.be/He9wbp-QbCA

The third testimonial is from Brittany:

I first discovered Daniel in the late spring of 2018. I quickly fell in love with how he conducted himself, the way he gave his messages, and all the love he put out in the world. I've lost a lot of people in my life and I think Daniel has

connected with every one of them in some form or another.

A couple weeks after watching Daniel, I lost my best friend, Brandon. Thinking back now, I think Daniel was put on my path to help ease some of the heartache I was feeling from losing Brandon. I had watched Daniel's live readings religiously for months, always interacting, hoping for a reading, but not being discouraged when it didn't happen. Then it did.

Daniel started saying a "BR" name like Brandon, and the number "33." (Bran's favorite numbers and number sequences were 33). Spirit kept bringing up a hammer and nails (Brandon was working in construction when he passed), the television show, Inspector Gadget (Bran's favorite TV show growing up), and a trumpet (which Bran played in middle school). Spirit also brought something up about the video game "Zelda," which was weird because Brandon's Facebook profile picture was a Lego picture of Link – the character from "Zelda™." When Brandon passed, our group of friends had a bunch of rubber bracelets made that we handed out to everyone. Daniel also brought that up too.

Our friend group always went to music festivals together on a regular basis, like yearly. I was so bent on making everything connect during my live reading and my nerves got the best of me. So, I couldn't link it up until after the reading was over. Brandon's mom and the rest of his family had spoken previously about having a bench dedicated to him, which Daniel had, of course, also mentioned.

There was a song that Brandon kind of made a parody

out of, something he always sang to another one of our friends, Matthew, who also got brought up in the reading. And the song was to the tune of "Chicken Fried," by the Zac Brown Band.

Daniel was able to pick up on Brandon's personality in the physical world as being very timid and very modest, which I thought was amazing. Everything Daniel said in my reading was amazing validation to know that Brandon was and is still with me, even down to mentioning a key that I had found the same day of my reading.

Brandon kept mentioning through Daniel that I was important to him and that I was important to his life. It was absolutely mind-blowing.

To further illustrate Spirit blowing my mind, my mom, who I lost when I was 17, came through as well. Our favorite flower, which was daisies, was brought up, along with a treasure chest that is filled with my mom's old costume jewelry. And also, through Daniel, she even mentioned how I got lost on the way to her gravesite. You can't make that up!

I've watched a multitude of live readings that Daniel has done for other people. My reading changed my life in a way I cannot explain. I was able to let go of a lot of anger and hurt that I was feeling. Although I'm still a little bit selfish, and I would like for both my mom and Brandon to still be here with me in the physical, knowing they're always with me in spirit, helps ease the pain so much. Daniel was able to give me that.

Daniel is always able to give everyone that feeling of

love and of never being alone. It was something I will never forget as long as I live. I could never put into enough words to express how thankful I am for Daniel and his gracious sharing of his gift with and for everyone else.

You can view Brittany's reading on my YouTube channel: https://youtu.be/TruylGKXQ2s

This next testimonial is from Jane, a mother who lost her son. This reading touches my heart, and I feel honored that her son was able to connect with me to bring Jane healing and peace:

I am writing to you to let you know how specific you were in my gallery reading with "Voice of Our Angels" group. For starters, when Daniel started to give free readings to all the moms/parents in the gallery, I believe my reading was about the third reading in. Daniel mentioned how the spirit was coming in with so much info and how he identified his name as beginning with a "TR." I believe he even said, "Travis," which is my son's name.

If Daniel had known my son in the physical world, it would make sense to have been prepared to have him come in strongly. I worried about Daniel's patience with my son even in spirit! Travis was always the one who would get someone's attention no matter what. He was this way since he was a young child.

From the very beginning, Daniel was spot-on. Daniel mentioned something having to do with his eyes, and I started

to tell him about something that I had received in my e-mail. It was something that pertained to Travis' eyes, and it was troubling me at the time, so much to the point I wasn't sleeping at night. I was beginning to tell Daniel about what I received, and he stopped me and said that Travis didn't want me to think about that or worry about it. That was such a relief to me! I had e-mailed the county medical examiner's office to request a copy of Travis's toxicology report and they sent me the entire autopsy report. I have yet to read the entire report. When I got to the second paragraph and they were describing Travis' eyes already having the grayish hue, it absolutely broke my heart. Travis had the most beautiful green eyes and I couldn't imagine them any different. Daniel provided me so much comfort by sharing that Travis wanted me to shut that thought down.

Daniel said that Travis mentioned his ex-girlfriend and said that he was so hurt when they broke up. I am not sure he had fully gotten over her. I haven't told this to many people, because people tend to judge and brand people too harshly, but Travis had gotten a Harley motorcycle a few months before his accident, and he had been hanging out with a local chapter of a biker club. He had been named a prospect within the chapter. When I first learned about this, I didn't like it at all, but after talking to some of the members, I was relieved to find out they weren't into breaking any laws or causing any serious trouble. They were an older group of men who took Travis under their wing, so to speak, and this was something my son was going to do whether I approved of it or not. He was 22, and he had already lived so much in those 22 years.

Everything Travis tried and went for, he did it 100%. He was a bull rider, played football, was very active in FFA and 4H. He had already worked at some interesting jobs and had no problem getting on with them. He had been hired by the LCRA as a temporary employee, and upon his return to work after the Memorial Day weekend, he was going on as a permanent employee, and he would have been making a very good living with excellent benefits. He never made it back the following Tuesday.

His motorcycle accident was on May 26, Sunday of that Memorial Day weekend. I drove up on his accident. I didn't even know it was him until I got closer to the intersection. It had just happened several minutes before I drove up.

I couldn't believe God put me there on that highway at that exact time. But my younger son said, "Mom I don't think you would have ever believed it if you hadn't seen for yourself." He was right. I would likely still be living in denial to this day.

The reason I mentioned Travis' involvement with the bikers is because I believe he wanted to get his ex-girlfriend's attention, maybe thinking this would impress her or something. Travis was a young man who wanted to be noticed and be the center of attention, but he didn't do it out of vanity. He didn't show off or act like a badass, but what he did do was show his devotion and commitment to whatever he was interested in.

Getting back to the reading, when Daniel started to mention something about the oven, I was absolutely floored. It actually took my breath away! Daniel asked if I left things in the oven, forgot about something I was cooking, and I said, "Daniel, I do this all the time." I keep a timer beside my bed that I set to remind me of when I need to check whatever I'm baking or cooking. Travis used to make fun of me, and when I would let a cake over-cook he would say, "Woman, I'm not eating burnt cake." Travis teased about how a woman's place was in the kitchen, and food should be tasty and cooked right. He knew I was more liberal, and I believe men are just as capable of cooking as women are. So, he would tease me and talk about how things were back in the 50s, but he would say it as if we were living back in those times!

Travis was always full of jokes and he was a quick thinker. He always had the quickest comebacks. He would leave me tripping over my own tongue while I would try to think of something I could come back with, which was usually something very lame. That oven comment was the very thing that turned Ed, my significant other, from a true skeptic into a true believer. Ed had known Travis since Travis was two, and Ed played a big part in helping me raise Travis. When he watched the video and heard Daniel say that, his jaw hit the floor. I said, "See, and you said, 'It's not real.'"

Daniel relayed that Travis told him to mention clowns, and I responded by telling Daniel that Travis was afraid of them. And my significant other immediately said, "No, Jane, it is because Travis was always a clown, even in grade-school."

I said, "That's right! But he still was also afraid of them!" I received calls at my job all the time from Travis' teachers telling me he would be coming home with a referral for acting out in class. It was never a dull moment with this child.

When he graduated high school, he had a total of 79 referrals written up on him. It wasn't ever for anything serious. It was all because he pushed the teacher's wrong buttons that day by saying something smart. And Travis thought he was funny, as did the entire class, but he picked the wrong days to say things.

Daniel was 100% accurate on everything in my reading. For Daniel to turn Ed into a believer says so much, because Ed is strong and stern in his beliefs. Daniel's reading really changed Ed that day.

These are the readings that remind me how blessed I am to have a gift that I can use to help others, especially grieving parents.

The next testimonial is from D'Lynn:

Daniel John happened to appear on my Facebook feed one evening. I listened for a bit to his Monday night reading and came back a few more Mondays. I was having some health issues that concerned me and I decided to book a private reading. My surgery was scheduled for January 8, and I was able to get a January 4 reading.

I was really hoping to hear from my parents, as I was

just really needing and wanting a hug from them. My wants were not the spirit's needs. The first spirit to come through was giving the validations of "Rick," "Richard," and number "47." Rich, my brother-in-law, passed away several years ago after many years battling liver disease, obesity, diabetes, and he was also on dialysis. "Rich" was easy to validate, but the number 47 threw me for a loop. I looked up Rich's obit, no number 47 for his death, birth, children. I thought, "Well he was a big race fan. Maybe it is his driver's number." Sure enough, number 47 is Richard Petty's number.

Daniel began sharing things like, "He's showing me a graduation and wants to thank you for going places with his wife." My nephew had just graduated from Officer's training in November. I met my sister in Quantico to attend the graduation with her. Rich wanted to make sure we knew he was there with us.

Rich also had Daniel talk about California. Jake is currently in California completing his training. There were several little validations Rich offered to ensure that it was him coming through. He mentioned his grandchildren by name, and events he had been a part of even though he wasn't physically present when they took place. He mentioned "his shirts" after his death. I had asked D'Anna, my sister, to send me some of his shirts. I had a friend of mine make teddy bears for their kids out of his shirts.

The final image Rich shared with Daniel is the one that brought me to tears. "He's showing me carrots. Does that make sense to you?" CARROTS? I attended my one and only Indy car race with Rich and D'Anna four months after the birth of my daughter. I had not drunk alcohol during, or since, her birth. The beers were SO cold and went down SO easy at the track and I tried watching the race. To make a long story short, I ended up getting sick on someone's truck tire and passing out in the back of Rich's car. He and my sister put carrots in my cleavage and took pictures. It was a memory we laughed about and joked about but never really shared with anyone. Rich would often say, "Got any carrots?' And we'd laugh, but our kids and my younger sister didn't even know the story behind the comment. That story was never written anywhere, and it has never been "posted" or shared. So, in my eyes, for Daniel to randomly mention carrots was impossible, and that "image" just solidified Daniel's ability.

Daniel then moved on to tell me he was seeing a "V." "Victoria," "Vaughn," a large "V" and a little "v." Vickie Vaughn is my cousin's name. Her father – my mother's brother – passed away December 31, and his last name was Vaughn. Daniel said, "This was a long death, wasn't it?" Well, yes, it was. My uncle had had a stroke a few years prior and had been in a nursing home for a long time. On most days he was not able to communicate with words. I had been able to see him in the fall of 2018, and his eyes lit up and the tears flowed. He was unable to clearly communicate to me, but I knew he was happy to see me. In mid-December he suffered another major stroke that left him unable to swallow or communicate at all, and he had a DNR order in place. Per his wishes, he was not given any heroic life support assistance.

My cousins all rallied around his bedside for over two weeks and were with him as he made his way to crossing over. Uncle Vaughn shared through Daniel that although he couldn't speak, he had heard everything that was said, and he was a part of those days. He showed Daniel "candy," and he wanted everyone to know he was okay and well. Daniel said that usually messages don't come so soon after someone has passed. He also said it was amazing to hear from Vaughn after only four days.

I didn't want to call my cousin immediately after my reading. I was worried her grief and mind might not quite be in a good enough spot to hear those messages. I just told myself to wait. A month or so, maybe even longer, after his passing, I called Vickie, ready to share with her what I was told in the reading with Daniel John.

I mentioned the vision, "candy," and she just began laughing and said, "We spent a whole day talking about candy!" She then told me about Uncle Vaughn's love for orange slices – the gummy type – which are sugar coated candy. Aunt Carolyn was so tired of orange slices, so Uncle Vaughn bought her some chocolate rum balls. Vickie laughed so hard at the purchase, and Aunt Carolyn responded with, "Anything, but those darn orange slices."

Then, during the bedside vigil, Vickie had brought in the same candy, but it was cherry flavored. She shared the orange slices and rum ball story with her siblings while they all ate the cherry slices.

Some weeks after his death, Vickie had begun to clear out the boxes of her dad's belongings and found the cherry slices. She wanted just one, but ended up eating the rest of the candy in the bag and got so sick to her stomach Not only did Uncle Vaughn sharing that information refer to the days of his dying, it was also a gateway to Vickie sharing with me what occurred even after the reading. Daniel's gift of giving comfort to others by relaying messages from our loved ones is awesome!

Our final conversation was about me, and Daniel said, "You're afraid of dying."

"No, I'm not afraid of dying."

"You're afraid of dying but you're not afraid of dying."

So, I then had to give some backstory to me wanting the reading. My family and I were in a horrific car crash in October of 2017. I had extensive injuries to my knee, pelvis, and hand. I had several surgeries, months of non-weight bearing, and lots of physical therapy. We knew from the first consultation for the first surgery that I would eventually need a hip and knee replacement.

July through December of 2018 was extremely painful for me. I needed the hip replaced and I was petrified I was going to die getting that surgery. I felt I'd been so blessed to have gone through all the other issues with ease and no real pain or setbacks. So, I felt that my luck was up, and this surgery would be my demise. I scheduled the reading with Daniel for a few days before the surgery. The pain became so unbearable we moved the date for surgery up to the earliest date possible. So, once I had the reading, I was no longer afraid of dying.

The poor nurse in the recovery room was gifted with hearing me cry, sobbing uncontrollably, and asking, "I am alive? You mean I lived? I'm really still here? Oh, thank you, God!"

In reality, Daniel nailed this on the head. I am not afraid of death. I am fearful of leaving my loved ones. He assured me, as I already know, when that time comes, I will still be with them all. Just as I have been okay and survived the passing of my loved ones. I am not, by any means, ready to depart this Earth, but my heart knows they will be okay. I also know that I leave my children, grandchildren, friends, and family, with memories, little pieces of me, and the gift of finding true joy in living.

I did not hear from my parents or grandparents in that reading. I'm starting to feel as though I don't need to, even though I just want to have one more moment with them. I have reflected on the idea that they left this world with me knowing how much I was loved, how proud they were of me, and they left me pieces of themselves that I bring out when I need a hug from them. I cook a favorite meal they cooked. I play a practical joke on someone. On Father's Day I recreate a picture of my dad, so that my tears are from laughing so hard versus tears from missing him so badly. Thank you so much, Daniel, for helping me realize so much peace and joy in my life!

This next reading was for Rebecca and her daughter:

On April 23, 2019, our grandmother passed away and our hearts have been broken ever since. She meant the world to us, and not having her here has been a huge adjustment. We had been tossing around the idea of going to see a medium and hoping to connect with her. I had been doing some research about who we could possibly go to and some people had given me some recommendations. And then I found Daniel on Facebook and watched some of his live readings before we set anything up.

We met with Daniel on November 23, 2019. My daughter, Brooklynne, and I had had many discussions about what to expect from this reading prior to going. Our last discussion was the night before we went, while we were in the Burger King® drive-thru, which was actually brought up in the reading.

When we walked into the room, the atmosphere was calm and relaxing. We weren't sure who, if anyone, was going to come through, as my grandmother is one of seventeen children. We started the reading, and right away Daniel was able to validate specific information.

My grandfather, William, came through and talked about horseshoes. I did not know what this was about, but my mother was able to validate that she used to play horseshoes with him when she was little. My grandmother also had a horseshoe hanging above her basement stairwell to catch good luck, but again, this was before my time.

After my grandfather passed away, my grandmother had a friend named Mary Lou that came around and helped my grandmother. My grandfather came through and said that he wanted to thank this person for stepping up and helping the family.

Daniel then brought up Pringles® and duck lips and wanted to know what that was about. My daughter immediately said that she had made duck lips with her Pringles® just days before the reading, at lunch while in school. Daniel then brought up seeing a gameboard. We then knew we were about to hear from the person we wanted to hear from, our grandmother, Raphaela.

We played Scrabble® with my grandmother on numerous occasions. I even took a picture of a Scrabble® game we had played with her and was thinking about printing it out prior to the reading. Daniel then brought up something about rainbows. We now have her table that she had on her back porch and she had made rainbow cushions for all the seats.

Daniel then brought up an angel. We had always hoped that my grandmother was Brooklynne's guardian angel, but angels were also validated by a figurine we had bought at the Corning Museum of Glass on Labor Day. We bought a little angel and agreed that we would put it out for Christmas for "Nonni."

My daughter had a very strong connection with Raphaela while she was alive, and this was also validated in the reading. Brooklynne still has a strong connection with her even now, and Daniel told her that she may have even been in past lives with her. We both believe in life after death and past lives, so this was a huge validation.

My grandmother was always worried about my uncle, Gary, who was her son. Daniel brought up that she wanted us to check on Gary to make sure he was okay. This would have been something she would have done while she was here.

Daniel also told us that he felt this reading was mainly for my daughter, Brooklynne. She has had a hard time dealing with the passing of my grandmother, as we all have. Through Daniel, our grandmother gave Brooklynne what we would call a "pep talk." Daniel told Brooklynne that her grandmother was watching over her, and that she is very proud of the woman she is becoming and the choices she is making. She also told Brooklynne not to let other people influence her choices and decisions. It was almost like Raphaela was right there in front of us and talking to us. It was amazing.

My grandmother came through with so much information and we were able to validate almost everything Daniel brought up in the reading. There were many things brought up that were before my time, but so many things that were current. I now know how everyone felt in all the readings

I listened to. I wish I could write everything that was brought up and validated, but we left the reading with comfort and peace, and knowing that she was okay and is still watching over us. Knowing that she is with our grandfather, and the rest of her family, gives us peace of mind. We know she is okay and that we will see her again. Thank you so much Daniel!

The next testimonial is from Connie:

My interest in mediumship came from the loss of very special people in my life who have passed. This included two of my children and my mother. For me, knowing that our loved ones are with us in spirit helps me through the grief process, and makes death a little less traumatic. While working through the grief of my 21-year-old daughter's death, I was on a road trip from Washington to Arizona, and I tuned into Daniel John's live show on 11-12-18. I was listening through a few readings when I realized my mother was coming through to bring me a message through Daniel.

My cell phone was losing the charge on the battery, so I pulled into a tiny gas station to get gas, purchase a few snacks (including Laffy Taffy®), and to call in to see if I could get through on the phone lines of Daniel's broadcast. The messages coming through were so precise, it was almost unbelievable. He mentioned my mother's name, "Dorothy," for starters. This is not a very common name.

Then Daniel actually said, "Laffy Taffy®," a specific kind of candy that I had just picked up off the convenience store's shelf at the gas station. That I succeeded to get through on my cell phone, which ended up dying two times while we were talking, was amazing. Following are a few messages that came through Daniel John from my mother that evening, along with the significance as to how they relate to me. Getting these messages from Daniel has forever changed my life and the way I look at death, dying, and the afterlife. What an honor to talk to and receive messages from my loved ones. My deceased mother had at least twenty different messages for me that night. I am starting with the most significant messages first, not in the order they came through in my amazing reading with Daniel:

Along with mentioning my mother's name, Dorothy, Daniel mentioned the number "73," which is my birthday month, July (7), and the number 3 (my birthday is 7/3).

Daniel said, "I have to talk about frogs." My mother loved frogs. She had frogs in her pond. She had frog sweatshirts and socks. We would catch frogs from the creek and bring them back to her pond. At her gravesite, a little green frog hopped out of the area that holds the flower vase on her tombstone. My father and I both knew it was her sending us a message.

Daniel mentioned "the little boy." This was my mother's first grandchild, my baby that passed away at birth. He also mentioned the number "8." My mother passed before my daughter was born. My daughter's birthday is 8-08-08.

Daniel asked, "Who is the 'C' name?" This is my name,

"Connie," or my mother's other granddaughter, "Cassie."

Daniel said, "Something of significance happened two years ago." Yes. My middle daughter was killed in a car accident two years prior. . .my middle daughter.

Daniel mentioned sunflowers. My mother grew huge, beautiful sunflowers. She loved to grow championship sunflowers from seeds she bought at the fair. My father had just given me a photo of him standing next to his beautiful sunflower.

Daniel referenced "throwing dollars in the air or making it rain money." My mother did this when we were kids. She would come home from winning money at Bingo and throw the money up in the air. It was always a highlight of her Bingo trips.

Daniel said, "Yahtzee®." My mom and I loved to play Yahtzee®. In fact, I packed the game in my car on the day of this reading.

Daniel brought up, "Laffy Taffy®." I had just purchased this candy at the store prior to going live on Daniel's show. This is validation that my mom is watching out for me and validation that she's here in spirit.

Daniel said something about a key. I had placed an extra key under a flowerpot, just hours before leaving on my road trip to Arizona, so friends could check on my place while I was gone.

Daniel also mentioned "flower." This referred to the flowerpot the key was under.

Daniel said something about "digging." My friend and I had planted a tree in memory of my daughter at my mother's gravesite.

Daniel mentioned the word, "flour." My mother, children, and I would all get together to bake cookies for Christmas. It was a very special event we did yearly. We would have big flour fights, getting flour on our faces and all over the kitchen. I took pictures of my daughters covered in flour. My mother also made the world's best fried chicken with a flour crust.

Daniel brought up "Pop Tarts®." My mom always had these on hand for my daughters. As well, a "V" name came up. My mother's best friend's name is Virginia. Daniel brought up Scrubbing Bubbles®. My mother had a big bathtub and always had Mr. Bubbles® and toys for the grandkids.

Daniel asked about Cracker Jack®. My mother loved Cracker Jack®!

So many messages came through. I am forever grateful to receive such beautiful validation that my mother is watching out for us from above. Thank you, Daniel John. I am forever grateful for you and the many people you help.

This last testimonial, from Deanna, touches my heart in such a special way. It feels like the reading was just yesterday, as it was so powerful for so many people:

After losing my 19-year-old son, Sean, I was searching for answers and wanted to know he was okay. I stumbled across Daniel John's live readings on a Monday night. I watched and was so amazed at his gift for connecting with spirits. I was questioning my faith and was wondering why God gave me my son only to take him away in 19 short years, leaving me without a future of exciting moments and memories to make.

I watched Daniel for a few months and rolled my eyes every time he spoke of God's love. Then one night he mentioned the number "47," and I knew it was Sean. Sean's social media was based around the number 47 and his friends have that number tattooed on their bodies for him. The clues kept coming to me: Tasmanian Devil, bubbles, Oreos®, diamond earrings, and, "Carl."

Daniel called on me and I explained my connections. I had called Sean the Tasmanian Devil because of his constant scatter-brain movements, bubbles were in his sister's bath as I was watching the video with her, we had just had Oreo® McFlurries®, I was wearing Sean's diamond earring, and Carl was their babysitter whom I had just seen the day before. As more came out I knew it was Sean. Daniel mentioned the name "Steve," who is my brother. He also mentioned chocolates in Sean's room, which I had just found in a stocking in his closet a few day ago, that had been left there from two years prior. Daniel mentioned the song, "My Girl," which Sean sang to me frequently.

I felt so much love and healing from that reading and from Daniel. It touched a part of my soul and changed my spiritual outlook. It helped me draw closer to God and to understand my path. My reading was such a blessing to my life. I found my smile and a little joy knowing that Sean was with me every day. Daniel continues to get the number "47" and sees things that are "Sean," and it brings me great peace.

My second reading was a paid reading on the 2nd anniversary of Sean's death. This reading was just as amazing. Daniel has a beautiful gift of connecting and bringing messages of love from the ones our heart yearns to hear from. Thank you, Daniel, for helping put this mother's broken heart into a mending state. I will forever be grateful for the peace and love you brought to me from my Sean.

You can view this reading on my YouTube channel: https://youtu.be/6tXU8TefF2g The reading starts at 22:50 in the video.

I hope by reading these testimonials, you have a better idea of what I do and why I do it. Reading these testimonials reminds me of how blessed I am to be able to use my gifts from God to serve Him by helping others. This is my life's purpose, and I thoroughly enjoy being able to connect with so many people on so many levels. I hope you enjoyed reading these stories. *Much Love! —Daniel*

Resources

Official Website: https://www.DanielJohnMedium.com

Official YouTube Channel: @DanielJohnMedium

https://www.youtube.com/DanielJohnMedium

Official Facebook Page: @DanielJohnMedium

https://www.facebook.com/DanielJohnMedium

Instagram: @DanielJohnMedium

https://www.instagram.com/danieljohnmedium/

Twitter: @DanielJMedium

https://www.twitter.com/danieljmedium

About the Author

Daniel John was raised Catholic and was "saved" in ninth grade. He is a devoted husband and the father of three beautiful children. When he was thirty-seven years old, Daniel experienced something profound. He realized that he had the ability to communicate with souls who have transitioned from this world to the next. At first, he was skeptical, and he was concerned about what was happening. However, after much experience, exploration, and listening to his heart, Daniel understood that mediumship was not only a gift from God, but a *request* from Him to use it to help others. Daniel is a Reiki Master and a certified spiritual medium who has a passion for helping people. Daniel's mission is to spread God's unconditional Love and help people live the absolute best lives they can live.

Made in the USA
Middletown, DE
19 September 2022